Transcend Aging

Stay Young Through the
Power of Your Beliefs

Anet Paulina
transcendaging.com

Transcend Aging

Stay Young Through the Power of Your Beliefs

Anet Paulina

Acknowledgments

The support and encouragement I have received from my many friends and kindred spirits has been invaluable – not just in creating *Transcend Aging*, but in navigating my life journey. Initially I intended to mention these wonderful folks by name, but realized it was almost inevitable that I would inadvertently omit someone. Instead I chose to include only the names of those who were directly involved in the creation of this book.

I would like to convey my appreciation to the following people: Kevin Post for taking the author photo, Dr. Bruce Lipton for reviewing part of Chapter 1, and Mary Ennis for permission to use the Elias information on energy centers.

To all who have shared with me their experiences on transcending aging, I offer a heartfelt "thank you."

Table of Contents

Preface

Here is the billion-dollar question: what is the secret to staying youthful regardless of chronological age? Is it even possible? The answer is yes, it is possible. Whether it is possible for *you* depends on whether you believe it is possible. The key to lifelong youth is simply believing – truly knowing – that the way you experience aging is completely up to you. As with many things in life, simple is not necessarily easy.

To those who may ask, "What is wrong with aging?" the answer is that there is nothing wrong with growing older, nor is age-related degeneration inherently bad. In some cultures, an elderly person wanting to look young would seem as ludicrous as an army general wanting to wear the rank of lieutenant. It is simply a matter of preference. If a person does not mind signs of aging, there is no need to address the subject. With matters such as health problems and loss of physical and mental functioning, however, the situation becomes murkier. These issues directly affect many aspects of life, not just physical appearance.

It was a surprise for me to discover there are folks who find value fulfillment in "negative" aspects of aging such as health problems and physical and mental decline. I prefer to avoid anything that entails dysfunction, clutter, or complication, and age-related degeneration involves all three. "Aging gracefully" typically means choosing to align with beliefs about degeneration and resigning oneself to their effects. If a person chooses such beliefs, I agree it is best if they accept the results. But people who make that choice are not morally superior to those who do not. If you are reading this book, I assume you prefer to remain youthful as you grow older, as I am approaching the subject from that perspective.

Although I believe the natural human lifespan is such that people could routinely live well over 100 years, I have no interest in extreme longevity. The point of life is not to exist in the same physical body for eternity, but to experience value fulfillment while we are here. My intention is to offer information that makes it easier for people to look, feel, and function the way they prefer as they grow older.

I would like to make it clear that I am not a medical professional and have no advanced degrees or certifications, nor do I claim to be an authority on health or anti-aging. (The term *anti-aging* makes me cringe, but I have not come up with a more positive yet succinct way to describe the avoidance of age-related degeneration.) If that is what you are looking for, there certainly is no dearth of professionals with a string of letters after their names who say they have solutions to the problems attributed to aging. My approach is much broader in perspective, as well as rather unconventional. It includes making use of various rejuvenating practices, but the core idea is to fundamentally alter the way we perceive aging.

My "credentials" are a lifelong interest and decades of study in health, fitness, nutrition, psychology, personal growth, and metaphysics, which led me to seek information about the keys to staying youthful throughout life. Mind-body interactions, intuition, energy healing, and psychic phenomena fascinated me long before they came into vogue.

At this point you may be wondering, *why does this woman think she knows more about aging than scientists and doctors do?* I would not phrase the question in quite those terms. I don't necessarily know more, but I am aware of some crucial factors that most anti-aging researchers remain oblivious to. Professionals with extensive medical or scientific training and certifications have a vested interest in limiting their ideas to the tenets of those belief systems. When faced with new information that fundamentally shifts the paradigm in one's area of expertise, it is natural to resist change, particularly when one has incorporated those beliefs so deeply that they seem like truths. I am fortunate to have the freedom to stretch the boundaries of currently accepted scientific dogma without jeopardizing my professional standing.

In 2000 I began making notes of my ideas, not with the intention of writing a book but simply because I thought the information might be useful at some point. As I watched the baby boom generation in their increasingly desperate quest to maintain or recover their youthful functioning and appearance, I realized that many people could benefit from what I have learned. In an exercise I sometimes use to clarify my priorities, I asked myself what I would most want to accomplish in the next year if I knew I had only one year left to live. The result is the book you are reading.

I have tried to strike a balance by offering information that does not perpetuate limiting beliefs yet aligns closely enough with commonly held views to be of practical value to most readers. Keep in mind that the health-related information I present is based upon beliefs – as is all such information, regardless of the source. The suggestions I offer regarding nutrition, fitness, and personal care are only tools; none is truly necessary for maintaining or regaining youthful functioning. They are methods that work within our belief systems to make desired physical changes, which can strengthen our trust that we have control over the aging process.

It was a challenge to decide how much belief-influenced information to include in the book. As a rule, I do not suggest that readers try to do things I have not yet accomplished myself. To maintain my own health and appearance, I still believe it is necessary to exercise regularly and eat nutritious foods. It would be disingenuous for me to tell others they can be healthy and attractive by remaining sedentary and eating junk food when I do not believe that would work for me. Also, heath-related actions can be used as a focal point for shifting energy and making physical changes. I have found that for some folks (especially those new to the metaphysical ideas), the practical suggestions are greatly appreciated.

Regarding methods and ideas I mention or recommend, keep in mind that these are only suggestions, which may not be effective or appropriate for every reader. Virtually every method works for someone, but no method works for (or appeals to) everyone. For the most part, my recommendations are based on what I personally have found to be effective. In a few cases I advocate methods that have not led to significant results for me, but I have direct knowledge of their effectiveness for other people and find the methods appealing because they are simple, economical, and virtually risk-free. It is important to remember that the true reason any method works is that it serves to help the individual shift her energy – and it is the shift in energy that actually caused the change.

Something I have purposely not done in this book is to provide scientific validation (study results or authorities cited) for all the information included. I chose this approach for two reasons. First, the determination of which facts require documentation is almost wholly dependent upon one's beliefs. When a person believes an assertion to be undeniably true, he sees no need to substantiate it. If he doubts the veracity of a statement, however, he is likely to demand validation. What complicates matters is that beliefs – even those considered to be basic truths – differ markedly among individuals. If I had attempted to validate every statement that someone might question, the Notes section would be almost as long as the text! Here is the guideline I used for providing documentation: For information I acquired directly from a specific source, I included an endnote to credit the source. For knowledge I have gleaned from multiple sources, I did not include an endnote.

The second reason for not providing supporting data for every statement that might be questioned is that including such corroboration would not really prove anything. Physicists have discovered that simply observing a subatomic particle changes its behavior. Since our physical reality is composed of subatomic particles, *everything* is influenced by the observer! Experiments and studies (including double-blind studies) are affected by the beliefs, perceptions, and expectations of the people involved. Therefore, even "conclusively proved" scientific findings may not be (and often aren't) any more valid than what your grandmother told you when you were a child. In addition, a person who does not want to believe something almost invariably will find (or invent) a way to invalidate it.

It is likely that some of the information in this book will challenge your beliefs, and it is meant to. Certain ideas may even seem preposterous to you. However, I encourage you not to let that stop you from making use of the information you find helpful. Personally, I have learned not to dismiss or discount everything a person has to offer simply because I disagree with him in certain areas. (In fact, in most of the books I reference and/or recommend, I do not agree with *all* of the author's ideas.) Each of us views the world through the filters of our own beliefs, and no one is infallible. Keep in mind that I am simply offering information, not trying to convince anyone that my ideas are the absolute truth. Use whatever is helpful to you and set aside the rest.

My intention is to help you become aware that there is an alternative to the dismal path you have seen so many people follow: progressive physical and mental degeneration leading to suffering, loss of function, and an unpleasant demise. Until now, scientists (and most of us) have viewed the physical body as much like an automobile you were randomly assigned – the best you can do is keep it running as well as possible as it gradually falls apart with age. *Transcend Aging* presents an alternative view: that by changing the way you perceive your body and realizing that you are in control of its condition, you can significantly alter the way you experience aging.

~~~

I plan on growing old much later in life, or maybe not at all.

—Patty Carey (American rodeo rider, circa 1900)

Part One:

Paradigm Shift

Chapter 1

The New View of Aging

~~~

Problems cannot be solved at the same level of awareness that created them.

—Albert Einstein (German physicist, 1879–1955)

Old Ideas About Aging

If you look at a newsstand, you may notice an interesting trend: magazine articles about dealing with aging are starting to outnumber those on weight loss. Several best-selling books promise lifelong youth, or at least the appearance of it. Advertising for anti-aging products is becoming increasingly prevalent. Companies promote skin-care products, hair-growth formulas, nutritional supplements, pharmaceutical drugs, and even pantyhose as solutions to the problems of aging. Anti-aging is a multibillion-dollar industry, and the trend is not likely to slow down anytime soon. In the United States, one of the most youth-oriented countries in the world, another person turns 50 every few seconds.

People who have reached an age where they start worrying about growing older generally fall into one of four groups. The first group consists of those who are resigned to the "fact" that they will degenerate with age and are trying to manage their growing health problems with medical treatments. They enjoy discussing their ailments and make frequent references to their declining mental and physical condition. To hear some of them talk, you would think they were 100 years old, when in fact they are closer to half that age. In the more extreme cases, the person's life revolves around doctor visits,

3

surgical operations, and prescription drugs. Their infirmities have become a significant part of their personality.

Members of the second group also believe it is natural to deteriorate with age but are determined to fight it with diet, exercise, nutritional and hormone supplements, skin-care products, cosmetic surgery, and anything else they think might help. They stay informed about anti-aging research and are eagerly awaiting the next scientific breakthrough or product that will provide "the answer." Compared to the first group, most members of the second group are in excellent health. Slim, fit, and active, they typically appear younger than their contemporaries. However, most of them work hard at it and spend a great deal of money on nutritional products, cosmetic treatments, and health club memberships. Some of these folks take so many pills every day that it is surprising they don't rattle when they do their aerobic exercise! (If it seems I am being unduly harsh on this group, it is because I was headed down that road until I broadened my views on health and aging.)

The third group combines the characteristics of the first two groups but is considerably less extreme than either of them. Members of this group expect to deteriorate gradually with age but try not to focus on it too much. They make an effort to take care of their health in conventional ways such as exercising regularly, eating nutritious foods, and using a few nutritional supplements. Beyond taking these basic measures, they do not believe there is much they can do to prevent the eventual breakdown of their body. Many are dealing with aging parents who require special care. The idea that they might end up in the same position as their parents makes them uneasy, so they try to avoid thinking about it.

The fourth group could best be described as "ageless." These folks understand that age-related degeneration is not inevitable; it is the result of aligning with a belief system. They do not accept the conventional idea that their future is dictated by genetics or external factors. Most members of this group use medical services or pharmaceutical drugs infrequently, if at all, and do not rely heavily on nutritional supplements or cosmetic treatments. This is not to say that many of them don't exercise, eat nutritious foods, and take care of their body. It is simply that they realize these external activities are not what keeps them healthy and youthful.

What is most impressive about folks in the fourth group is that (regardless of their genetics) they are not aging at the same rate as their contemporaries. "My genetic heritage suggests I would have female reproductive problems such as breast cancer and fibroid [uterine] tumors, probably resulting in a hysterectomy by age 45," said Marcy, who was born in 1952. "My family history also indicates I'd have heart disease, chronic depression, and sinus trouble, and that I would be overweight in middle age. I have none of these health problems, and I'm not overweight," she noted. Marcy has no dental problems and has not been to a dentist since age 14. "The last time I had a gynecological exam, the nurse said I was the oldest patient they had seen all day, and also the healthiest," remarked Marcy, who looks considerably younger than most people her age. Although she has been nearsighted since childhood, she does not need bifocals. "I went to the eye doctor the other day and he said I have very 'youthful' eyes. Even my astigmatism has cleared up," Marcy added.

It is not uncommon for those in the fourth group to be taken for 10 or 15 years younger than their chronological age. When I first met my friend John, he mentioned that he was born in 1953, but he looked so much younger that I thought he must have said 1963. I was so sure I had misheard him that I asked him to repeat himself three times! John is in excellent health and almost never gets sick (even with minor illnesses), needs no vision correction, has only a few strands of gray hair, and has not been to a doctor in years. He takes no drugs or nutritional supplements other than a vegetable-based green drink and an occasional vitamin C pill. John exercises only moderately (some calisthenics and aerobic exercise a few times a week), yet he can walk and climb at high altitudes with greater endurance than most people much younger.

While writing this book I met a beautiful, youthful, and vibrant woman of indeterminate age. Since she obviously took good care of herself, I guessed Barbara to be in her early fifties, although she gave the impression of someone younger. Later I learned she was in her mid-sixties, in excellent health, and had not had cosmetic surgery. Barbara is not in denial about her age. She loves being a grandmother, but also likes to dress stylishly and engage in active pursuits like dancing and skiing. In every way but chronologically, she is younger than many people who are 20 years her junior. A key difference between Barbara and many of her contemporaries is that she does not think of herself as old.

I am not the only one who assumed Barbara was much younger than her chronological age. A male friend of hers, eight years her junior, said one of his clients saw a picture of the two of them and asked if Barbara was his daughter! At a grocery store, Barbara requested the senior citizens' discount (for customers age 60 and older) and the clerk laughed, assuming she was joking. In a reverse version of being "carded," Barbara was asked to produce her driver's license to prove she was entitled to the discount. The astonished clerk exclaimed, "You look great! I sure hope I look that good when I'm older."

At this point you may be wondering what is the secret of people in the fourth group – have they discovered the fountain of youth? In a way, perhaps they have. Those in the fourth group do not align with the conventional belief that age-related degeneration is inevitable. They realize that how they experience growing older is determined primarily by their own beliefs and choices.

New Paradigm

According to conventional beliefs about aging, we are on a countdown clock to degeneration and the best we can do is use external methods to try to hold things together as long as possible. Medical science views the human body as fundamentally defective – if left to its own devices, it will deteriorate with age until it can no longer function. Anti-aging researchers study the mechanics of the aging process: DNA transcription errors, cells that fail to replicate after a finite number of divisions, and organ function that deteriorates over time. The goal is to discover what goes wrong that causes age-related degeneration and develop methods of outsmarting the body to prevent these changes from occurring.

Within a narrow context, this view seems to be correct, but it is only part of the story – a very limited part. The scientific perception of the human body as a flawed piece of machinery that breaks down over time flies in the face of the spiritual view of humans as perfectly created beings. A person is not just a physical body and brain with consciousness tacked on as an afterthought. The mechanistic view of the human body is inaccurate: consciousness creates the physical body, not the other way around.

The burgeoning anti-aging industry has been operating from a flawed premise: that age-related degeneration is built into our DNA and cannot be altered or avoided except by using external methods. The truth is that cell behavior is controlled not by our genes, but by our perception of the environment. In other words, we control the aging process.

It is not necessarily that anti-aging researchers are barking up the wrong tree; many of the trees they are looking in actually do contain something. The problem is that they are focusing on the trees without being aware of the forest. For instance, some theories point to free radicals as a primary cause of age-related degeneration. (Free radicals are oxygen molecules that have lost an electron and stabilize themselves by taking an electron from a nearby molecule, causing cell damage.) What the researchers fail to recognize is that we don't age because our bodies produce too many free radicals – we produce too many free radicals because we believe in aging.

This is not to say that scientific discoveries about aging or recommendations for extending youthfulness are necessarily invalid. Given our present mass beliefs, the most efficient way for many folks to stay youthful longer may be to apply some of the scientific information in practical ways. I see nothing wrong with using methods that are natural to the body and do not involve a great deal of inconvenience or expense. It is important to understand, however, that it is possible to function optimally into old age without medical intervention.

The fundamental reason for age-related degeneration is not that the body is defective; it is that we essentially program it to decline with age. This is not to say that we would continue to look exactly as we did at age 25 if we simply altered our beliefs about aging. The body is a reflection of our inner self, which changes in every moment. I doubt that many people would want to remain as they were in their youth, with the same attitudes and maturity they possessed at 25. As we become more experienced in life, it is natural to project a physical image that appears older.

Older, however, does not necessarily mean less attractive and desirable! Some people may say, "I would love to be able to keep the wisdom, knowledge, and skills I have acquired, yet look like I did when I was 25." But would they really? I suspect that most adults with a fair number of years of experience want to be recognized as a little older because an older countenance tends to draw more respect. Youth certainly has its charm, but the defined features of a full-fledged adult can be more attractive than the somewhat unformed features of a younger person.

Change is natural, but we do not have to start falling apart when we reach a particular age. The primary reason people deteriorate with age is that they believe they will. Our physical form is a manifestation of our nonphysical self, and it follows our expectations. If authorities such as scientists and doctors tell people they will degenerate because they have reached a certain age, they are likely to believe it – and will do just that.

Our beliefs and perceptions cause electrical and chemical reactions in our bodies. If you believe your body is breaking down, you will cause it to break down. It is much like when a physician tells a patient he has three months left to live and the patient dies precisely three months later, or when a witch doctor puts a curse on a person and it works. (The "witch doctors" in our society typically have medical degrees!)

Your body is not a vehicle you inhabit; it is a creation of your nonphysical being that reflects your personality. Facial wrinkles (expression lines) can be an external manifestation of automatic reactions – habitually doing the same things and repeatedly making similar choices. An inflexible body can be a physical representation of becoming set in one's ways. Many people become less mentally flexible as they grow older, hence the stiffness and loss of physical flexibility experienced by so many older adults. It can happen the other way around as well: if we become more mentally flexible, our physical flexibility can improve. I am living proof that this is possible. When I was younger, I was quite rigid in my attitudes and physically inflexible as well. Not surprisingly, I disliked stretching exercises. Contrary to what is expected to occur as we age, my physical flexibility has increased considerably, and I now enjoy stretching and yoga.

Many people consider the words *mind* and *brain* to synonymous and believe the mind resides in the brain. In truth, the human mind exists in the energy field that surrounds, permeates, and in fact creates our physical body and brain. In addition, the mind (and the personality) does not die when the body ceases to function.

The mind-body effect is not hocus-pocus; it is an actual physiological process. If you doubt that your perceptions and beliefs affect your body, think about what happens when you

9

hear something upsetting. If, for example, someone told you one of your loved ones was in a serious accident, you would experience immediate physiological changes. Your heart would start beating faster (raising your blood pressure and pulse rate), your breathing would quicken, and you might break out in a sweat. Nothing really happened to you, so what caused all these changes? Simply your perceptions, beliefs, and thoughts!

We typically do not realize that what we think and speak can affect our body. Each time you say something like, "I forgot where I put my car keys again; I must be getting old," you are reinforcing a belief that tells your body you expect it to deteriorate. Such reinforcement has a cumulative effect, which is why the people who think and talk the most about getting old are the ones who seem to age the fastest. Their thoughts and words reveal the person's beliefs and concentration of energy. The trick is to catch yourself when your attention is focused this way, which allows you to alter your energy.

Most of us have grown up in an environment where we not only see people deteriorating with age; we are taught that it is a normal and unavoidable part of life. Our brains and bodies, like obedient soldiers, respond to our beliefs and give us precisely what we ask for.

Think of your body as if it were a corporation: your mind is the president, the organ systems are the divisions, the organs are the departments, and the cells are the workers. The workers, departments, and divisions try to do a good job and satisfy the president. The president, however, is unclear about what she wants and sends mixed messages to her employees. She expects them to do something (deteriorate with age), but complains when they meet her expectations. In addition, she often fails to supply the workers with the proper materials (nutrients and water) to run the factory, adequate rest breaks (sleep), and activity periods (exercise), yet she expects them to continue performing at an optimal level and becomes angry when they do not. The president then calls in experts (healthcare professionals) to find ways to deal with the "problem" employees. In truth, the workers are not the problem; they are simply doing what the president indicates she wants them to do.

Fortunately, it does not have to be this way! When we realize that our beliefs and perceptions are the primary cause of physical and mental degeneration, we can choose to align with different beliefs. Over time, such a shift will make a dramatic difference in how we experience growing older. In the near future, perhaps turning 50 will be considered not the beginning of old age, but the threshold of the second stage of our youth.

Biology of Belief

All this talk about aging and beliefs sounds great, you may be thinking, but why isn't there scientific evidence to substantiate it? Ah, but there *is* scientific evidence. Cellular biologist Bruce H. Lipton, PhD, has shown that the health and behavior of our cells is controlled not by our genes, but by our environment – or more specifically, by our perception of the environment. Although Dr. Lipton's research is not directed toward the study of human aging, I recognized that his research is pertinent to this subject. It should be noted, however, that the conclusions drawn in this book about the relationship of Dr. Lipton's findings to human aging are my own.

Bruce Lipton's work first came to my attention when I attended his presentation at a conference in 1999. As it ended, I sat dumbfounded and declared to a friend, "This presentation has changed my life." The statement was melodramatic but true. From studying metaphysics I had learned that we create our own reality, but there was a part of me – the logical, rational part – that needed to understand *how*. Finally, in terms I could comprehend, was an explanation that filled the gap. And it came from a highly credible source: a cellular biologist with impressive credentials. Bruce Lipton received his doctorate from the University of Virginia, has served on the faculty of several medical schools, and spent five years as a research fellow at Stanford University's School of Medicine.

Dr. Lipton's research revealed that scientists have been making logical conclusions based on a fundamentally flawed premise: that the characteristics and fate of a life form are dependent upon its genes. If the brain is removed from an organism, the organism immediately dies. Removing a cell's nucleus (which contains the DNA and hence the genes) does not kill the cell, which proves that the nucleus is not the cell's command center or "brain," as is commonly believed.

According to Dr. Lipton, "If the nucleus truly represented the brain of the cell, then removal of the nucleus would result in the cessation of cell functions and immediate cell death. However, experimentally enucleated [with the nucleus removed] cells may survive for two or more months without genes and are capable of effecting complex responses to environmental and cytoplasmic stimuli. Logic reveals that the nucleus *cannot* be the brain of the cell!"[1] This finding proves that genetic determinism (the idea that the characteristics of an organism are determined by its genes) is a myth.

Through studies on cloned human cells, Lipton recognized that the cell's "brain" is actually the cell membrane. The cell membrane, which separates the cell from the external environment, was the first biological organelle (structure within a cell that performs a differentiated function) to appear in evolution, and it is the only organelle common to every living organism.

Cell membranes are composed primarily of phospholipids (major structural lipids, or fats) and proteins, including special proteins called integral membrane proteins (IMPs). The two types of IMPs are receptors, the "sense organs" of the cell, and effectors, which carry out cell behavior. According to Lipton, "Receptor IMPs 'see' or are 'aware' of their environment, and effector IMPs create physical responses that translate environmental signals into an appropriate biological behavior. The IMP complex *controls* behavior, and through its effect upon regulatory proteins, these IMPs also control gene expression.... The IMP complexes provide the cell with 'awareness of the environment through physical sensation,' which by dictionary definition represents *perception*. Each receptor-effector protein complex collectively constitutes a 'unit of perception.' "[2]

Scientists traditionally believed that receptors responded only to molecules (matter), but new research has shown that receptors also respond to energy signals. "Conventional medicine has consistently ignored research published in its own mainstream scientific journals – research that clearly reveals the regulatory influence that electromagnetic fields have on cell physiology," notes Lipton. "Pulsed electromagnetic fields have been shown to regulate virtually every cell function, including DNA synthesis, RNA synthesis, protein synthesis, cell division, cell differentiation, morphogenesis, and neuroendocrine regulation. These findings are relevant, for they acknowledge that biological behavior can be controlled by 'invisible' energy forces, which include *thought*."[3]

One of Bruce Lipton's fundamental concepts is that a cell can be in only one of two modes: growth or protection. "Growth" in this context can also be described as love, openness, and expansion; "protection" equates to fear, closure, and contraction. When we perceive our environment to be dangerous, our cells go into protection mode and fail to use available resources to rebuild, repair, and renew. Growth and protection also can be associated with anabolism (rebuild and repair processes) and catabolism (breakdown processes) According to the metabolic theory of aging,[4] degeneration occurs when the body's catabolic processes exceed the anabolic processes. We all start out as highly anabolic, but conventional science says the ratio naturally changes as we grow older: catabolic processes become increasingly dominant, resulting in the degeneration we call aging.

From Dr. Lipton's research, I learned that whether we are in growth or protection mode depends on our perception of the environment. Applied to the metabolic theory of aging, this means that developing an increasingly catabolic metabolism as we grow older is not inevitable. Anabolism equals growth. If we perceive our environment to be safe, our cells are in growth rather than protection mode, resulting in a metabolism that is more anabolic than catabolic. Therefore, we – not our genes – control the rate at which our body ages.

Bruce Lipton's research (and his enthusiasm for sharing his discoveries) is playing an important role in advancing our understanding of the nature of reality. For more information about Dr. Lipton's work, see his book, *The Biology of Belief: Unleashing the Power of Consciousness, Matter, and Miracles*,[5] and website (brucelipton.com).

Your Body Reflects Your Beliefs

Every aspect and function of our body is a manifestation of our inner self. For instance, the physical sense of vision reflects how we view the world. Many (not all) people become farsighted as they grow older. A possible reason for this vision change is revealed in the word *farsighted* itself, which means planning for the future. Farsighted people may be focusing on the future more than on the present, and this habit is reflected in their physical sense of vision. Another reason some older people lose the acuity of their near vision could be that increased life experience enables them to see the big picture more clearly than the details. But perhaps some folks are failing to perceive the true characteristics of things because they believe they already know what they are like. They distort the details, perceiving things as they expect them to be rather than as they are.

Another condition associated with physical aging is inflammation, an immune system response that is implicated in numerous disorders such as arthritis, diabetes, cancer, heart disease, and Alzheimer's disease. Inflammation has long been known to play a role in allergies and asthma, as well as autoimmune diseases such as lupus and multiple sclerosis, in which the immune system attacks the body's own tissues as if they were foreign invaders.

The immune system is the body's defense system. Like all defense systems, it is activated when a threat is perceived. Whether the threat is real or not is immaterial; it is the perception of danger that triggers the immune response. Therefore, it is conceivable that the fundamental precipitating factor in many diverse age-associated disorders is *fear*. In our society, it is typical for people to live in a state of low grade, constant fear. Most news reports and much of our advertising is fear-based. Prolonged exposure to fear-inducing stimuli may activate the immune system and cause inflammation, which eventually damages the tissues enough to result in an obvious disease state.

The physical effects of beliefs and expectations were clearly demonstrated in an experiment performed by psychologist Shlomo Breznitz at Hebrew University, Jerusalem.[6] Breznitz had several groups of Israeli soldiers march 40 kilometers (about 25 miles), but gave conflicting information to each group. Some groups marched 30 kilometers and then were told they had to march 10 more. Others were told they would march 60 kilometers but actually marched only 40. Some groups were allowed to see distance markers; others had no external means of gauging the distance they had walked. After the soldiers completed the marches, Breznitz measured their blood levels of stress hormones and found significant differences among the groups, even though they all had walked the same distance. The soldiers' hormone levels clearly reflected their beliefs and perceptions about the distances they marched rather the actual distances.

The findings of this experiment have significant implications regarding how we experience the aging process. Our beliefs about what to expect as we grow older not only have tangible, measurable effects on our physiology, they actually define our experience of aging. A woman who worked with vision-impaired folks told me that many blind people stay younger-looking than their contemporaries. Possibly this is because they cannot see other people's signs of aging and therefore do not assume they will experience the same changes.

In his book, *Past Fear and Doubt to Amazing Abundance*, Stephen Hawley Martin shares a thought-provoking experience he had in a convenience store.[7] While waiting in line to buy a bottle of beer, he noticed a sign that said, "We ID Under 27 Years of Age." When Martin reached the counter, the clerk requested his identification. At first he thought she was joking, but the clerk told him she was quite serious, so he produced his driver's license. The woman gasped in amazement when she saw his birth date, which revealed that he was 55 years old – more than twice the age required to show identification to purchase alcohol!

Not only did the clerk think he looked no older than 27, Martin realized he felt just as young as he had at that age. Pondering the incident later, he recalled that when he was 25, he read about a study that found that people who took large doses of vitamin E did not show any measurable signs of aging. Thinking that vitamin E was a veritable fountain of youth, he bought a bottle and had continued taking it ever since, believing the pills would keep him from aging. Years later he saw another article that said vitamin E supplements could not be proved to retard aging, but he dismissed the study results and continued taking the vitamin. Although subsequent research has shown that vitamin E supplementation does appear to lower the incidence of cardiovascular disease, cancer, and other health problems, it clearly has not prevented its users from showing any signs of aging. After the incident in the convenience store, Martin realized that very likely, the vitamin E supplement had worked for him largely due to the placebo effect.

Martin's experience with vitamin E supplements is similar to what happened to me when I took gelatin for my fingernails. At age 10, I had weak fingernails that cracked and peeled easily. I wanted my nails to be strong so I could grow them long like my aunt, who had beautiful nails. When I asked her for advice, she told me she drank gelatin daily to strengthen her nails. I started drinking the nasty stuff every day as well, and within a few months my nails became strong and were growing faster. I continued taking gelatin for about three years and even after I stopped, my nails stayed strong and grew quickly. By that time I had come to think of myself as a person with naturally strong nails. I now prefer to keep my nails fairly short, but when I want to grow them longer, I can do so easily. Years after my gelatin-drinking days, I learned that consuming gelatin has no effect whatsoever on fingernails – the substance is just incomplete, inferior protein. It was my belief in the gelatin that made my nails strong, not the substance itself.

Stories about the placebo effect abound. Psychotherapist Robert M. Williams relates a poignant one in his book, *PSYCH-K: The Missing (Piece) Peace in Your Life!*[8] In the late 1980s, an Eastern European family that had immigrated to the United States sent a large "care package" to their relatives back home who were having difficulty obtaining basic supplies. Communications were slow, so it was nearly six months before the family received a letter from the appreciative recipients. The relatives said they were most grateful for the medication, which had helped numerous family members experience significant improvements in their health. The medication was running low, and they were fervently requesting more. Those who assembled the care package were puzzled because no one remembered having sent any medication. Ultimately they discovered that the "medication" actually was a popular candy! "Please, please send more of the Lifesavers," their relatives entreated. "They made such a difference!"

A less heartwarming (but even more amazing) account is shared by Alan Cohen in his book, *I Had It All the Time: When Self-Improvement Gives Way to Ecstasy.*[9] A train-yard maintenance man accidentally locked himself in a freezer car; and his lifeless body was found by his coworkers the next day.

He had scribbled on the wall the words, "cold... getting colder... freezing." His writing provided clues to the cause of his death, which otherwise would not have been apparent – because the freezer car was not working. The man died not due to external circumstances, but because he *believed* he was freezing. Such stories demonstrate how beliefs can save a person's life – or end it.

Why Does Aging Occur?

In summary, here are four basic reasons we experience the changes we call aging:

1) The belief and expectation that the physical body and brain degenerate as we grow older.

2) Habitually existing in protection rather than growth mode: fear, closure, and stifling one's life force energy.

3) Belief in the effects of health-related factors such as nutrition, exercise, and exposure to things that are considered harmful.

4) Changes to our inner self that are reflected in our physical form: we perceive ourselves as older, therefore we look older.

The good news is that we can directly influence the first three factors, reducing undesired aging-related changes to a minimum. The changes due to the fourth factor can manifest as subtle alterations rather than the obvious signs of degeneration we have learned to expect.

Chapter 2

Shifting Beliefs About Aging

~~~

But I was so much older then; I'm younger than that now.[10]

—Bob Dylan (American singer, songwriter, and poet, 1941–)

Consciousness Shift

There is a shift in human consciousness occurring now, a movement to a state of broader awareness. Part of this shift is recognizing that what we consider to be absolutes – the concepts we have based our world upon – are simply beliefs we choose to align with, not unalterable truths. In other words, we made the rules and then forgot we did, and now mindlessly follow these rules as if we had no other choice. How tenaciously we cling to our narrow definitions of what we believe constitutes reality!

Many people sense this shift in consciousness but do not really understand it. Rather than recognizing that virtually all of our institutions (including science and religion) are based upon belief systems, they are creating additional beliefs to explain the consciousness shift. Those who abandon traditional religions for New Age alternatives are typically just swapping one set of beliefs for another. They still are looking for something outside themselves to provide "the answer," but now it is astrology instead of psychology, a guru in lieu of a priest.

Beliefs and Truths

In our reality, there are no absolute truths. (That statement itself is an absolute, but it is the best I can do within the limitations of our language.) In my view, black and white do not really exist. The color we call white is actually a very pale shade of gray, and the color we call black is an extremely dark shade of gray.

Virtually everything we consider to be a truth is actually a belief. We take on most of our cultural and familial beliefs in early childhood – automatically, as if by osmosis. Typically we are unaware that they are beliefs; we think of them as principles that define the way things truly are. These fundamental beliefs become our personal truths: the basis on which we determine whether something is good or bad, true or false, or right or wrong.

Contrary to what most of us have been taught, beliefs are not a matter of right or wrong; they are simply preferences. The key to transformational personal growth is realizing that our truths are actually beliefs, which means they are subject to change – and to choice. If you are unhappy with something (in this case, age-related degeneration or the expectation of it), you can choose to align with a different belief, and this will change your experience.

Many age-related beliefs are commonly accepted as truths. How often have you heard (or made) statements like, "He looks good for his age," or expressed surprise that a 70-year-old woman ran a marathon? We may want to believe that getting older means getting better, but our thoughts, words, and actions reveal our true beliefs. We commonly hear people make statements like, "I forgot where I parked my car; I must be getting senile." Individuals of all ages do absent-minded things, not because they are stupid or their brain is degenerating, but because they are not paying attention (a subject that merits a book of its own!). When I can't find my car, it is not because I forgot where I parked; it is because I didn't notice in the first place.

You Control Your Body

We have the innate ability to maintain our physical bodies in a healthy and attractive state without outside help. However, it can be difficult to alter a strong belief without some evidence that it is possible. When people make lifestyle adjustments that result in desirable physical changes such as increased energy, greater flexibility, better skin tone, and loss of excess fat, it helps shift their beliefs about what is possible. Such methods also can serve as a focal point for channeling energy to make changes. Yet regardless of drugs, supplements, exercises, cosmetic treatments, or anything else you may try, if you believe aging means deterioration, ultimately you will deteriorate.

In altering my beliefs about aging, I have found it helpful to hear about people who have made physical changes not considered possible according our culture's belief systems. If you have difficulty accepting the idea that we can influence our physical bodies in profound ways, consider the implications of the following dissociative identity disorder (DID) (formerly known as multiple personality disorder) cases discussed in *The Holographic Universe*.[11]

A person diagnosed with DID has multiple distinct personalities, at least some of which are not aware of all the others. Not only are the personalities different, there can be dramatic biological differences among them. Allergies, for instance, often are present in only some of the personalities. In one DID case, all but one of a man's personalities were allergic to orange juice and would develop a severe rash if they drank it. If the man switched to the nonallergic personality, the rash would immediately start receding and he could drink orange juice with no adverse effects.

Not just allergies, but also the effects of alcohol and medication can vary greatly among personalities. A DID patient who is drunk may become sober instantly by switching personalities. If an adult personality is given an adult dose of medication and a child personality takes over, it sometimes results in an overdose. A DID patient may have to carry several pairs of eyeglasses due to substantial differences in vision among various personalities. In some women, each female personality has her own menstrual cycle. Even more surprising, some personalities have different eye colors and voice patterns. (According to speech experts, even expert actors cannot alter their voice patterns.) Other conditions that may change from one personality to the next include scars, cysts, color blindness, diabetes, epilepsy, and left- and right-handedness.

The fact that physical characteristics and conditions such as eye color, left-handedness, and diabetes can change from moment to moment in a DID patient means that physical characteristics are subject to change, not "hardwired" into our physical bodies as we have been led to believe. If a DID patient can eliminate an allergy or metabolic disorder, why can't anyone? When you realize that humans have the ability to change their eye color, it is not so hard to believe you can alter or avoid things like facial wrinkles, fat deposits, and failing vision.

In addition, avoid getting caught in the trap of believing you are likely to inherit whatever disorders "run in your family." Genetic heritage may give you tendencies for certain traits, but you choose whether to actualize them. As Marcy (mentioned in Chapter 1) remarked, "I decided a long time ago that I was not like everyone else in my family and that their physical problems had nothing to do with me – and they haven't. Even though my genetics probably has all the markers for those disorders, I decided not to align with the belief that I would inherit the family ills, so they never were activated." It is noteworthy that Marcy chose to stop having routine medical checkups and diagnostic tests. As she put it, "I realized that if I kept going for the exams, eventually they would 'find something.' "

For any belief, there are almost countless possible influences. Even if you hold that belief, you are not subject to *all* of these influences. Most of us have a belief that the human body degenerates with age, but no individual expresses all the potential influences of this belief, which include numerous life-threatening diseases. If they did, they would be dead! Given the current mass beliefs, it would be challenging to hold *no* belief in age-related degeneration, but it is helpful to remember that each of us has a choice of the influences of this belief. You, like Marcy, can decide not to be influenced by beliefs about diseases that "run in your family" or are given attention by the news media.

For me, this realization was very powerful. I had been feeling discouraged that after years of studying these concepts, I still felt it would be virtually impossible for me to entirely avoid age-related degeneration. Then it dawned on me that although I hold this belief, it is apparent that I am not experiencing most of its potential influences – and the influences I am experiencing are relatively minor. When I realized I do not have to dispense with the belief entirely in order to avoid its most deleterious effects, I felt a sense of freedom.

Reversing Aging

Is it possible to reverse aging? The answer essentially is yes – but not if you think of it in those terms. I can almost guarantee that a person who tries to reverse aging in the conventional way of thinking will be disappointed. We can grow younger in terms of physical appearance and health (and many people have done so), but trying to reverse a process that most of us fundamentally believe goes in only one direction is unlikely to be successful. In so-called reversal of aging, what occurs is that the person starts believing the age-related conditions are not permanent and inevitable. She realizes she does not have to manifest these conditions and starts creating her body in a way that does not express them. The person is not reversing anything; she simply is creating her body in a different form than she did previously.

Anet Paulina

A common reason for wanting to reverse aging is that looking older often is equated with loss of attractiveness. It was somewhat of a revelation for me to realize that I don't value youth so much as I do beauty. Physical beauty (be it in nature, humans, or objects) is an outward expression of balance and harmony, and a desire for balance is a preference of mine. Youth, however, does not necessarily engender beauty, nor is it a prerequisite for it. Every day – in every choice you make – you can put your energy into beauty and harmony, and these characteristics will manifest in your physical form, regardless of your age.

Models of Youthfulness

In the Far East there are numerous accounts of people who have maintained or regained youthful appearance and functioning well into old age. Increasingly, such folks are showing up in Western cultures as well. Long-term practitioners of yoga typically remain more youthful than their contemporaries, sometimes markedly so. In one such case, a yoga instructor (an African-American woman who appeared to be in her late thirties) was speaking to middle school students about the practice of yoga. Many of the students seemed unreceptive to her ideas; some were almost belligerent. When she asked them to guess her age, they intended to insult her by guessing she was in her fifties. When she revealed that she was over 70 years old and had been practicing and teaching yoga for more than 30 years, the students gave her their rapt attention for the rest of the presentation.

Another example of perennial youthfulness is John, a physician who emigrated from Hungary to the United States in 1966 to escape Communism. When he was practicing medicine in Europe, the patients he considered old generally were those close to 100. This attitude has served him well, apparently. A few years ago John went to a discount store in search of a specific item. A store employee said he knew were

24

to find it and led John to the appropriate aisle. The box was on the bottom shelf, and the employee apologized for not being able to bend down far enough to lift it. "When you get to be my age," he said with a sigh, "you just can't do all things you used to do." John assured the employee that he did not mind lifting the box himself and did so easily. Out of curiosity, he politely asked how old the man was. "I'm 53," was the reply. John was stunned. "If you don't mind my asking," added the employee, "how old are *you*?" John recovered his composure enough to tell the man that on his next birthday he would be 80 years old.

Numerous well-known individuals are remaining youthful well beyond age 40, which used to be considered "over the hill." Fitness expert Jack La Lanne (born in 1914) is legendary for the feats of strength and endurance he performed even at ages when many of his contemporaries were in nursing homes. Actress Sophia Loren, a movie star since the 1950s, remains stunningly beautiful. Media personality and producer Dick Clark, dubbed "the oldest living teenager," has been recognized for his youthful appearance as much as for his 50-year career of achievements in the television industry. Susan Lucci, best known for playing the gorgeous and conniving Erica Kane on the television soap opera *All My Children*, is as lovely in her sixties as she was decades ago. A younger example is actress Rene Russo (born in 1954), whose perennial youthful beauty is reportedly not due to cosmetic surgery. Likewise, actress Jennifer Beals, who starred in the 1983 movie *Flashdance*, is even prettier now than she was in her twenties.

Celebrating Birthdays

The term *aging* itself is almost synonymous with degeneration. Whether applied to a human being or an inanimate object, it implies loss – loss of function, usefulness, attractiveness, and desirability. It would be helpful to use another word (at least in your own mind) to describe growing older. *Evolvement* is a good alternative, since it implies advancement in a positive way. You are not aging; you are evolving!

Our culture categorizes people by age so much that it is hard not to be drawn into conventional thinking, particularly when you have a "landmark" birthday with a number ending in zero. I have found it helpful to decide on alternate meanings for these occasions before they occur. Turning 50, for example, does not have to mean you are over the hill. It can mean you no longer have to follow rules or conventions that are not to your liking (provided that you are willing to face potential consequences, of course). At this point in your life, you may feel you have learned enough to know what is right for you and to make your own decisions. You probably will opt to continue to follow traffic rules and such (there's that consequences thing), but you don't have to act like a person your age is "supposed" to act. You can dress like a teenager, ride a roller coaster and shriek like a banshee, stay up all night yakking with your best friend, or whatever else strikes your fancy. If you don't limit yourself to behaviors expected from people born in the year you were, you will be less likely to fall into the conventional pattern and start manifesting the signs of physical and mental degeneration that also are expected to occur when people reach certain ages.

Shortly after a landmark birthday, I had an employer-required medical checkup and was amazed at the number of negative suggestions I received from healthcare professionals. They recommended numerous diagnostic tests, implying that (based only on my birth date and gender) I was vulnerable to all sorts of dire diseases. With each refusal of an unpleasant-sounding test (can you believe I turned down an offer for a free colonoscopy?), I said to myself, *This doesn't apply to me. I am not going to manifest these conditions.* I chose to react to their warnings in much the same way as if they had given me a lecture about not stealing from the company: I listened politely, but knew it was not relevant to me. Developing cancer is not something I will do in this lifetime unless I am ready to leave physical life in a manner that allows for preparation time, in which case I probably would choose not to undergo medical treatments anyway. Disease and degeneration do not just happen to us; they are a choice of experience based on our beliefs.

This is an appropriate place to mention that when I use the word *choice* regarding illness, injury, and other hardships, I don't mean that a person chooses these problems the way he might choose an ice cream cone: "Yes, I'd like a serving of lung cancer, thank you very much. And while we're at it, can you throw in a little arthritis, some diabetes, and maybe a car accident on top?" The individual most likely did not want to develop a disease or have an accident, but it was the choices he made – the things he chose to believe and express in energy – that manifested physically in these ways. Nor are manifestations that are considered health problems inherently bad, although they may be unpleasant and inconvenient. (A cyst or tumor, for example, could be an outpicturing of vibrant creative energy.)

A remark sometimes made to a person having a birthday is, "You may think you're old, but you should be happy – right now you are the youngest you will ever be." This assertion is not really true. For example, a person born on 6 January 1950 had his fiftieth birthday on 6 January 2000. On that date, his 20-year-old self (who was "born" in 1970) turned 30 years old. His 50-year-old self, however, was just "born" that day. Therefore, his 20-year-old self is actually older than his 50-year-old self! The self we create in each moment is younger than all of our supposedly younger selves. There is some distortion in this idea because in truth, everything is created in the present moment, including our 50-year-old self, 20-year-old self, and newborn self. Viewed in the context of our beliefs about chronological time, however, this idea can be useful for reframing limiting ideas about aging.

Clichés about the benefits of aging ("You're not getting older; you're getting better") can sound hollow to those who are experiencing undesired effects of age-related beliefs. Yet there truly are advantages to growing older, and not just the frequently mentioned benefits of wisdom and experience. Some people dread growing older because of the undesirable changes they believe will occur in their body and mind. When we are old enough to have proved to ourselves that these fears are unfounded, we no longer have to dread the future. In this regard, older people have an advantage over younger ones.

Perhaps we need to adjust our ideas about what is considered the prime of life. Believing that we peak in our twenties is like believing a rose peaks when it is just a slightly opened bud! Because this is how we view life, most people live like roses that start drying up long before they fully bloom. If we altered our idea of the prime of life to age 50 rather than 25, it would make a tremendous difference in the quality of our lives.

Thinking back to when I was in my twenties and thirties (which many people consider the "peak" ages) it is apparent that I was not yet at my best in many areas, including physically. Probably even 50 is too young to be considered the prime of life. It is ludicrous that some organizations classify people who have reached 50 as senior citizens. The current human lifespan is about 120 and likely will increase. By my calculations, that means a person turning 60 is just entering middle age.

Shifting "Old" Beliefs

Following are some ideas to help shift your beliefs about aging. If you do nothing else but follow these suggestions, it can make a significant difference in how you experience growing older.

- Pay attention to everything you think and say regarding aging, and identify the underlying beliefs you are expressing. When you catch yourself joking that you had a "senior moment," for example, it reveals that you expect your mind to deteriorate with age.

- Offer yourself alternatives to negative age-related thoughts and statements. For instance, you may notice that an acquaintance looks older than she did the last time you saw her and then start wondering if you look older as well. Remind yourself that how she looks is a reflection of her beliefs and that you can choose differently.

- Start thinking of your body as self-renewing – as regenerating rather than degenerating. Avoid monitoring yourself for age-related changes. The more attention you give to such features, the more are likely to appear. Focus instead on the aspects of your appearance that make you feel good. On some days you will perceive that you look and feel young; on other days it may be the opposite. Your physical body is a manifestation of your inner self, which is constantly changing. The way you look and feel today will not necessarily be the way you look and feel tomorrow (or five minutes from now) unless that is what you create.

- Rather than categorizing yourself by your age group, start thinking of yourself as a generic adult – a grownup of indeterminate age. Quite simply, you are a physically mature human being rather than an infant, child, or adolescent – and you will remain in that category until you leave this life, regardless of how many years of experience you have. When you define yourself as a 48-year-old or a person over 60, it is hard not to be affected by conventional beliefs about a person that age.

- Drop the habit of mentioning your age frequently or even thinking about it often. When you tell people your age, they perceive you through the filters of their beliefs about a person that age and reflect that image back to you. If you prefer not to disclose your age and someone asks how old you are, you can respond with, "I stopped counting after __," using any figure that strikes your fancy. (Numbers over 100 or under 20 have the greatest humorous impact.) A response I particularly like is, "I stopped counting after 20. Once I got past all my fingers and toes, it was just too confusing."

- Avoid using age or infirmity to justify your choices. People who cite age or limiting physical conditions as an excuse are headed down a slippery slope that ultimately can lead to degeneration, even incapacity. When you don't want to do something, be honest about it with yourself and others. If friends want you to join them on a hike but you would rather stay home and read a book, don't say, "I would love to go, but my back has been acting up again" or "I just can't keep up with you young folks like I used to." When people make such excuses, they are giving themselves reasons to degenerate. Just be honest and say you don't feel like going.

- If you enjoyed an activity in the past but do not care for it now, give yourself permission to eliminate it from your life. If you force yourself to continue, you may manifest an injury or illness that will give you a reason not to do it anymore.

- When celebrating birthdays (yours and other people's), refrain from making age-related jokes that reinforce pessimistic ideas about growing older. Avoid buying birthday cards with negative age-related messages, particularly those that refer to loss of attractiveness or mental function. These supposedly humorous greeting cards may seem inconsequential, but they reinforce beliefs that lead to degeneration.

- If you receive an email with a list of jokes about aging, press the delete key. Eventually your beliefs will have shifted to the point that pessimistic messages and age-related jokes no longer trigger negative feelings in you. Until you reach that point, however, it is best to avoid exposing yourself to them.

- Avoid paying much attention to the mass media. The media (especially advertisements) reinforces beliefs about age-related degeneration and poor health, as well as fears about crime, terrorism, and disasters. Watching television can be most insidious because it puts people in a state of high receptivity in which they essentially are programmed to accept the sensory input. Once you are aware of this form of programming, you can make a conscious choice not to subject yourself to it.

Advantages of Being Older

Consider the phenomenon I call the Antique Paradox: objects such as furniture and cars are commonly believed to become more valuable over time, while human beings are considered less useful and desirable as they grow older. It would be more constructive to believe the opposite! Typically we hear a lot about the disadvantages of being over 40 and little about the positive aspects, which include much more than greater wisdom and experience. Here are a few you may not have thought of:

- Your self-definition has evolved to the point that you are much more the person you want to be than when you were younger.

- If you have not developed health conditions that typically manifest in childhood or early adulthood (such as type 1 diabetes or multiple sclerosis), it is unlikely you ever will.

- If you are not schizophrenic, you probably never will be. The onset of schizophrenia is typically before age 30. When it occurs after 40, it tends to be milder.

- Regardless of the physical attributes you were born with, if you have taken good care of yourself, you probably are healthier and more attractive than most of your contemporaries.

- Having evolved past the generic plumpness of youth, your facial features are more defined and unique.

- You feel freer to express yourself because there is not as much pressure to blend into the herd to be accepted.

- While you may choose to continue your education in a formal setting, you never again will have to go through primary or secondary school.

- Women after menopause no longer have to deal with the hassles of menstrual periods, premenstrual tension, birth control, getting pregnant, or worrying about getting pregnant.

- When you are 25, you don't know yet if you are an annual (a plant that grows for only one season) or a perennial (a plant that lasts indefinitely). By the time you are in your forties, you realize you can choose to be a perennial.

- You no longer have to dread turning 40, 50, 60, or 70 because you are there now and things are better than you expected.

Part Two:

Mind Matters

Chapter 3

Developing Awareness

~~~

We don't see things as they are; we see them as we are.
—Anaïs Nin (French-born writer, 1903–1977)

Paying Attention

Our fast-paced society teaches us to focus our attention outwardly, as if what goes on inside is of little importance. In fact the opposite is true: we create internally and project our creations into the external, physical world. The internal and external creations happen simultaneously; it is not "cause and effect" in the way we typically think of it. Actually it is a correspondence: our inner and outer worlds move in sync. When we don't pay attention to our inner world, we go through life like a blindfolded artist indiscriminately slapping paint on a canvas. When the artist looks at her creations, she often is disappointed (sometimes even horrified), yet it never occurs to her that she could remove the blindfold and pay attention to what she is painting while she is painting it.

Many of us feel that our busy schedules and the demands of daily life leave no time for introspection, yet we feel chronically stressed and dissatisfied. It is easy to fall into the habit of living with mediocrity, assuming our lives will continue that way and not thinking about it much. Essentially, we are on "automatic pilot" to a destination we have not consciously chosen. This seems to happen most when we are very busy, paying attention to matters that are urgent but not important. Some people live their entire lives this way, creating urgency so they won't have the time or energy to address deeper subjects.

How can we change this unfulfilling way of living? The key is to develop the habit of paying attention to what you are feeling, thinking, saying, and doing – and to identify your motivations. A method I have found helpful is to frequently ask myself, "In this moment, does what I am engaged in (doing and/or thinking) help fulfill my intentions?" If not, I ask myself what would be more beneficial. Paying attention to the way you feel about something helps determine if it is in harmony with your intentions. This method presupposes that you are aware of your intentions, which is not always the case. Nevertheless, most of us can easily identify at least our short-term intentions.

When someone is described as "self-conscious," it usually is meant in a derogatory way. In fact, being self-conscious is beneficial – it means you are paying attention to what you are feeling, thinking, and doing. Typically what is meant by self-conscious is "self-critical," which is a different state.

Thought, Emotion, and Intuition

Our emotions, physical senses, and inner senses (including intuition and impulses) are avenues of communication that provide feedback and guidance on what we are creating. If you feel bad, it is a signal to alter what you are doing or thinking by making new choices. Pain (physical or emotional) is impelling you to make a change.

As a general rule, if something feels bad, stop doing it! Most of us follow such impulses regarding physical matters. If we are sitting in an uncomfortable chair, for instance, we will move. With emotionally uncomfortable or painful things, however, often we endure them far longer than is necessary. If a hailstorm was raging, would you stay outdoors even though you were being pelted by hailstones? Of course not, or at least not for long. Yet if something nonphysical is hurting us as much as the hail, often we go out in the storm and keep going back for more despite the bruises we receive. While it can be an interesting experience to be in a hailstorm briefly, there is little point in continuing to subject oneself to something painful.

The function of *thought* is to translate and interpret communications from the emotions and senses. Thought is often used inappropriately, to override rather than interpret communications. There are countless times when I've had a feeling or intuition that later turned out to be correct, but I "logic-ed" myself out of it and failed to take advantage of the insight. An example of using thought to override a communication is when a person is driving and has an impulse to take an alternate route. Rather than following the impulse, he talks himself out of it because the other route is longer and has more stoplights. He continues on his usual way and encounters a traffic jam due to road construction or an accident.

The habit of using logic to contradict inner communications is like a one-person version of the humorous question, "Are you going to believe what you see or what I tell you?" We tend to believe what we tell ourselves rather than what we perceive with our inner senses and physical senses.

It is widely recognized that in making decisions, our thoughts (rational mind) and emotions are sometimes in conflict. *Should I follow my head or follow my heart?* is a common dilemma. Following the head often means making a choice that seems logical but feels wrong. Following the heart entails choosing what we want at a particular time, which may not be the best choice.

In decision-making, there tends to be three things at play: logic, emotions, and intuition. Logic takes into account the facts we are aware of, information provided by our physical senses, and knowledge from past experiences – all of which is filtered through our beliefs. Emotions also are strongly affected by beliefs (for example, if we believe something will hurt us, we are likely to be afraid of it), as well as by desires and preferences. Although intuition often is described as a feeling, it is quite different from emotions. Intuition is a communication from our inner self that is meant to steer us in the appropriate direction to fulfill our life intentions.

Intuition sometimes conflicts with logic, emotions, or both. Logic is a useful tool, but it operates from limited information: only the facts we are consciously aware of (or paying attention to) at the time. Intuition takes into account information we may not be aware of, as well as the broader view based on our fundamental life intentions. Emotions typically reflect what we want at a particular time, which may not be the best choice for us. Intuition usually is subtle, a small voice deep within you. Emotions, which tend to be out front yelling loudly, can easily drown out intuition's quiet voice. (This is not to say that emotions are not necessary or useful; they are an important avenue of communication. It is a question of appropriateness.)

There have been times in my life when I have done something I did not consciously want to do and that did not make sense rationally, yet I felt compelled to take the action. Later I would discover why, and it would be obvious that I had done the right thing at the right time. For example, on several occasions I felt compelled to go somewhere I did not consciously want to go, with no logical reason for doing so. While driving or walking to the destination I had (seemingly) not chosen, I would be thinking, *Why am I going here? I have no reason to go here, and I don't even want to go!* Almost invariably, it turned out that I would "happen" to find something I had been looking for or meet someone I needed to talk to. I suspect I have avoided some auto accidents that way as well.

It takes practice to become skilled at distinguishing intuition's subtle communications from emotion's blatant signals. Individuals perceive intuition in diverse ways. It can manifest as an inner feeling, a thought or mental "flash," a voice in one's mind, or a physical sensation. Some people experience all these forms of communication at different times. Over time, you will become familiar with your own "language" of inner communications. The challenge is to connect with your intuition and listen to it even when it conflicts with emotions, logic, or both. In my experience, that little voice has never been wrong.

Making Choices

When you need to make a decision and are having trouble distinguishing intuition from emotions and logic, it is helpful to use an efficient method for choosing the best option. For me, a reliable method is the "pick the choice that looks brighter" technique. I imagine myself doing what I would be doing if I made choice A, and then I imagine the results of choice B, and so on. Usually one scenario looks brighter than the others, which lets me know it is the best option.

Another method I use is to formulate a yes-or-no question that captures the essence of the dilemma. I then imagine the words *yes* and *no* in different colors, in block letters on a white background. Usually for me the *yes* is red and the *no* is blue, but you may prefer other colors (perhaps green and red, like traffic lights). At first both words appear fairly small, but then one of them expands until it dominates the picture, revealing the answer.

When making a choice that involves a moral dilemma (deciding the right thing to do under particular circumstances), I ask myself if the alternative I am considering promotes love and unity or fear and separation. If it is the latter, then it probably is not the best option.

Meditation

Sometimes I feel as if my conscious mind is a barking dog that needs to be put in the backyard so I can hear what my inner self has to say. Meditation (focused awareness) is an effective way to enhance this inner communication, as well as to reduce stress and achieve deep relaxation. Following a regular practice of meditation can be challenging for those who grew up in Western cultures, however. The most well-known form of meditation (maintaining a thought-free state for an extended period) requires the ability to calm and focus the mind, which is not easy for everyone. Rather than trying to stop your thoughts, concentrate on something such as a word (mantra), an image, or your breath.

Rather than considering meditation to be one more thing you have to do each day, think of it as a way of giving yourself (and your mind) a rest. The more enjoyable you can make your meditation practice, the more likely you will be to continue it. If you are unaccustomed to meditating and tend to have trouble staying still, begin with short sessions and gradually work up to longer ones. If you cannot manage a 15-minute meditation period, try meditating twice a day for just 5 minutes each time. Forcing yourself to meditate for longer than you are comfortable will make you dread the next session, which is why I don't recommend meditation practices that involve sitting in an uncomfortable position or forcing yourself to keep your eyes open. Meditation should help achieve a state of focused awareness that is relaxing, not unpleasant.

Practicing meditation does not necessarily involve sitting motionless in the lotus position with a blank mind. The type of meditation known as *mindfulness* (paying attention to what you are doing in the moment, without having extraneous thoughts) may be easier for some people. If sitting still does not work for you, try an active form of meditation such as walking, bicycling, or performing repetitive tasks like housecleaning.

Neurochemicals

In addition to benefits such as deep relaxation and enhanced concentration ability, a regular meditation practice has beneficial effects on hormone levels in the brain and body. Meditating increases the level of endorphins (peptide hormones that bind to opiate receptors, reducing pain and increasing feelings of pleasure and comfort) and also reduces blood levels of cortisol, the major adrenal cortex hormone. An integral part of the "fight or flight" response, cortisol is secreted in greater-than-usual quantities in response to stress. When levels of the hormone are elevated for sustained periods, it can be detrimental to the body and brain.

The adrenal glands also produce another hormone believed to play an important role in aging: dehydroepiandosterone (DHEA), a steroid that can be converted into other steroid hormones such as estrogen and testosterone. DHEA has been dubbed the "youth hormone" because it is believed to counteract some of the biological effects of age-related degeneration. This hormone is considered a biomarker for aging because levels generally drop in proportion to a person's age. DHEA levels are high in young people but tend to decline markedly as a person gets older. A 70-year-old, for instance, may be producing only one tenth of the DHEA he produced at age 25. Low levels of DHEA are directly correlated to depression, Alzheimer's disease, heart disease, and a host of other age-associated disorders.

The adrenal glands secrete DHEA in inverse proportion to cortisol: the more cortisol, the less DHEA. Logically it would seem that reducing the production of cortisol would lead to increased levels of DHEA, and apparently it does. Several studies have shown that people who practice meditation have significantly higher DHEA levels than nonmeditators of the same age. In one study, researchers found that people who practiced Transcendental Meditation for 20 minutes twice a day had DHEA levels typically found in nonmeditators 5 to 10 years younger.[12]

DHEA can be taken in supplement form, and many people have used it without apparent ill effects – at least so far. Although it often is sold along with vitamin and herbal supplements, DHEA is a hormone – a drug, not a nutrient. With virtually all hormones, taking a supplement eventually results in the body lowering its own production of that hormone. I find it difficult to believe this won't happen with DHEA as well. There are no truly long-term studies of the effects of DHEA supplementation because no one has been taking it for more than a few years. Those who decide to try DHEA supplements should have a blood test to determine their current level of DHEA before deciding on a dosage. Also, taking the hormone intermittently rather than continuously makes it less likely that the body will become habituated to it.

Brainwaves

Brainwaves are categorized by frequency. *Beta* (a frequency of 12 to 30 Hz) is the state most of us are in during the active part of our waking day. When we are relaxed, our brainwaves slow into the *alpha* range (8 to 12 Hz). Beyond alpha is the *theta* brainwave (4 to 8 Hz), which is common in children but typically occurs only during twilight sleep, dreaming, and very deep relaxation in most adults. The slowest brainwave, *delta* (0 to 4 Hz), occurs during deep sleep.

At any given time a person has a mix of brainwave frequencies, but one type generally dominates. The predominant brainwave for most people in the waking state is beta. When we are very relaxed or in light meditation, our brainwaves slow into the alpha range. Very experienced meditators (such as Zen monks) sometimes reach the theta state during meditation, but it is uncommon for most adults to be in theta except when they are falling asleep, awakening, or dreaming. In the theta state, our beliefs and habit patterns are more malleable and we can easily access deeper portions of our consciousness.

Float Tanks

Developed in 1954 by John C. Lilly, MD, a float tank (also known as a flotation or isolation tank) is a lightproof, sound-insulated chamber that contains 25 centimeters (10 inches) of Epsom salt-infused water warmed to 34.2°C (93.5°F), an average person's skin temperature. Lying in the tank allows a person to float effortlessly, with the entire body fully supported and free from the effects of gravity, light, and sound. The benefits of the float tank have been studied and applied in diverse areas including health care, athletic and fitness training, education, meditation, and spiritual development.

Particularly for those who find it challenging to meditate, regular sessions in a float tank can help immensely in achieving deep relaxation and altered states of consciousness. Floating allows most people to easily reach a state in which theta brainwaves are predominant. In addition, floating substantially increases the body's level of endorphins while decreasing the level of stress hormones, and the altered hormone levels can continue long after a float. To find a float tank center, perform an Internet search on the phrase "where to float."

Breathing

Far more attention is given to health concerns such as diet and exercise than to the seemingly simple activity of breathing. Considering that humans can survive for weeks without food and days without water, this attention seems misplaced. Without air, we would perish in minutes. Yet many people are shallow breathers who rarely take full, deep breaths. One of the reasons physical exercise is so beneficial is that it requires us to breathe deeply.

Breathing Practice

It is worthwhile to spend a few minutes every day focusing on your breath. A good time to do this is after exercising or before meditation. Following is a simple breathing technique that most people (those without serious respiratory problems) find easy and refreshing.

1) Sit or stand comfortably with your back straight. Throughout the exercise, keep your mouth closed.

2) To a slow count of four (about four seconds), take in a full, deep breath through your nose. Do not strain or try to force in as much air as possible; just inhale until your lungs feel comfortably full. As you inhale, your chest and abdomen will expand.

3) Hold the breath for four seconds.

4) Exhale through your nose to a slow count of six (about six seconds).

5) Hold for two seconds.

6) Repeat the four-step cycle 10 times.

7) As you become accustomed to this exercise, you can gradually increase the length of time between breaths (steps 2 and 4), but never to the point that you are straining yourself.

Alternate Nostril Breath Cycles

Throughout the day, our bodies move through alternating two-hour (approximately) cycles that are conducive to either rest or activity. In the active phase, the brain's left hemisphere (connected to the right side of the body) is dominant. In the passive phase, the brain's right hemisphere (connected to the left side of the body) is dominant. The precipitating factor for these cycles seems to be the breath. The right nostril is more open in the active phase; the left nostril dominates in the passive phase.

At any given time (presuming you don't have a respiratory blockage), you can tell which nostril is dominant simply by pressing your finger against one nostril to close it, breathing only through the opposite nostril, and then reversing the process to see which side is more open. When the right nostril is dominant, it is a good time for exercise, eating, and engaging in other active pursuits. Cycles of left-nostril dominance are more appropriate for rest, meditation, and passive pursuits, as well as for drinking fluids. Normally the cycles switch about every two hours, but occasionally (due to stress or depression) you can become stuck in one mode for several hours.

When you are in a passive phase and need to be active, or are in an active phase when trying to rest, you can coax your body to switch cycles. Lying on your right side tends to close the right nostril and open the left one, so it is a good position for sleep or relaxation. Lying on your left side tends to have the opposite effect: it closes the left nostril and makes you feel more active. You also can manually close one nostril for a few seconds to encourage the opposite one to take over, breathe that way for a few seconds, and then release the nostril and breathe normally. Repeat this pattern several times until the desired nostril becomes dominant. Rather than intentionally shifting nostril dominance, however, it is best to honor your body's rhythms and match your activities to the existing cycle. Reserve methods of altering nostril dominance for times when you have been in one mode for an extended period.

Challenges to Awareness

Procrastination

It is crucial to discern the difference between appropriate timing and procrastination. Sometimes it doesn't feel like quite the right time to take an action because it is not the best time. In other instances the time does feel right, but we delay taking the required action due to inertia.

Each time you think about doing something but don't do it, you devote time and energy to the task without accomplishing anything. For instance, if a chair in your bedroom is piled with garments that need cleaning or mending, every time you see it you tell yourself, *I really should deal with those clothes.* You carry this nagging thought with you and it consumes some of your mental energy. The same applies to the dirty dishes in the kitchen and stack of papers on the hall table.

The solution to ending this waste of mental energy is simple: do the jobs that are nagging you. If it is not practical to complete a task immediately, then schedule it as you would any other appointment. For repetitive tasks, schedule a block of time every day, week, or month. In addition, don't stop working when you have almost completed a job – a mostly done task is still an undone task. Completing the job allows you to cross it off your list and release the energy associated with it.

The more obstacles that exist between you and an activity, the less likely you are to engage in that activity. For example, you join a health club and plan to work out three times a week. Each time you want to exercise, you must change into the appropriate clothing, drive to the health club, sign in at the front desk, go to the locker room to store your gear, and stand in line to wait for the equipment. All this and you haven't even started to exercise yet! However, this principle can be used to your advantage when trying to break a habit. To cut down on smoking, for instance, buy only one pack of cigarettes at a time. You may find that when you want a cigarette, you don't want it badly enough to go to the trouble of driving to the store and standing in line.

Handling Habits

Most people have what I call *global characteristics*: patterns expressed in many diverse aspects of their lives. For instance, I tend to do things a little at a time. I sip water throughout the day, eat several small meals in lieu of two or three large ones, and pay bills promptly rather than waiting until they accumulate. A friend of mine prefers to do things in batches: he drinks large quantities of water infrequently, eats two meals a day, and pays bills twice a month. Global characteristics can be broad ranging and include traits such as perfectionism, impulsiveness, procrastination, overindulgence, thoroughness, and neatness.

There is a physical, electromagnetic reality to habits and patterns. It is possible to take on other people's habits in the same way we tend to follow an existing path rather than creating our own path. It is easier to do something when someone else has done it before, even if you are not aware that they have.

I realized the pervasiveness of habit patterns when a friend visited me for a few days. The bedrooms in my house were upstairs, with the master bedroom on the left and the guest bedroom on the right. My friend was annoyed at herself because every time she climbed the stairs, she automatically turned left even though she knew she should turn right. Finally we realized the cause of her seemingly illogical behavior: she was following the strong "energy path" to the master bedroom that was created not only by my partner and me, but by the couple that had lived there before us.

The birds that frequented my backyard provided another demonstration of the tendency to follow established patterns. The songbirds liked to eat seeds from the hanging feeder, as did the larger birds. In their pursuit of the sunflower seeds mixed with the millet and corn, the larger birds were scattering the songbird food on the ground. Also I noticed the songbirds usually left the feeder when the larger birds arrived. I decided the best solution was to buy the songbirds a special feeder that was too small for the other birds to access. I kept the old feeder and filled it with sunflower seeds for the larger birds. This seemed to be an ideal setup. The songbirds would have their own feeder, and the other birds could have as many sunflower seeds as they wanted.

However, I soon observed that the songbirds did not use the new feeder but continued to visit the old one, ferreting out the last of the songbird food from among the sunflower seeds. It was frustrating to watch them scrounging for the few seeds left on the ground and in the old feeder, when the fully stocked songbird feeder was right next to it. To access this cornucopia, the songbirds had only to notice the new feeder and find the openings. Ultimately I resorted to radical measures: I removed the old feeder and put the new feeder in its place. Finally the songbirds started using the new feeder. After allowing them to practice their new habit for a few days, I hung the old feeder on the other side of the pole for the larger birds.

It occurred to me that the songbirds were acting much like humans do: continuing to follow established patterns even when they no longer serve us. Locked into our old habits, we fail to notice new opportunities that are right in front of us, ripe for the picking. Too often, we investigate these opportunities only when outside circumstances force us to change (when the old feeder is taken away, so to speak).

Here is an effective strategy for changing a habit (in this example, smoking): Regardless of how long you have been smoking cigarettes, you become a nonsmoker the instant you truly, unequivocally decide to be one. After that, even if you experience an occasional lapse and have a cigarette, you still are a nonsmoker; you simply are engaging in behavior that is not characteristic of you now. When you view yourself as a nonsmoker, your behavior and choices conform to your new self-image.

Chapter 4

Conscious Creation

~~~

You create what you concentrate upon – not what you think,
for your concentration is not based in thought.
Your concentration is based in your beliefs.[13]

—Elias (energy personality essence)

Creating Our Reality

Introduced into popular culture by Jane Roberts's Seth books, the expression "you create your own reality" has become a New Age catchphrase.[14] Yet even those who follow these philosophies can find it hard to believe we create everything in our world, nor do we understand how. Because we don't understand how we create, we ascribe creations we are pleased with to good luck or divine intervention. When something happens that we don't like, we attribute it to bad luck or punishment from some deity. Yet in every case, we are the creators of our own experience. There really is no such thing as luck, and no deity is directing the day-to-day events of our lives.

I used to believe there were two kinds of people: those who made things happen and those whom things happened *to*, and that I clearly was in the latter category. Eventually I discovered this view was flawed. Each of us is responsible for creating everything we experience. I will be the first to admit, however, that manifestations often don't seem to be under our control! Many things happen in life that we would not have chosen deliberately. The question of what an individual did to "bring something on themselves" is irrelevant. If a person is suffering, the natural response is compassion. Of course they created the situation; each of us has created every bad (and good) thing we have experienced. The "why" question is for the individual to answer, if he cares to.

In a spiritual discussion group, I had a lively exchange with a woman who took issue with my assertion that we create our own reality. Her son had been killed in an automobile accident several years earlier, and she thought I was saying she was responsible for his death! It surprised me that someone could interpret "you create your own reality" in this manner. I explained that being in the accident (regardless of who appeared to be at fault) was her son's choice, but she chose to participate in the experience with him. The woman insisted that if it were up to her, she never would have chosen that experience. By this point, she was demanding an explanation from me. I knew she worked as a grief counselor and had significantly helped many clients accept a loved one's passing. I suggested to her, "Suppose one of your intentions for your life was to help people deal with grief and loss. Your son, for his own reasons, chose to disengage at an early age. Wouldn't it make sense for you to choose to share that experience with him? If you hadn't gone through extreme grief yourself, you probably would not have become a grief counselor – and would lack the direct experience that enables you to relate to others who are dealing with the loss of a loved one." This explanation made sense to her.

Energy Follows Attention

The axiom "energy flows where attention goes" is one I have found to be true. Paying attention to something focuses our energy there, and energy is what causes physical manifestations and draws things to us. Following are two stories that illustrate how moving one's attention can result in tangible changes in areas that seem to be beyond our control.

When mobile phones started becoming widely used (but notably, before I had one myself), I sometimes noticed cars being driven badly because the driver's attention was focused on a phone conversation. After this occurred a couple of times in quick succession, I started feeling annoyed at just the idea of people talking on a phone while driving. Soon I was encountering mobile phone-using bad drivers several times a day! The more attention I paid to such drivers, the worse the problem became.

Finally I decided to address the issue. My solution was to force myself to stop judging drivers who were using mobile phones. When I noticed such a driver, I reminded myself that the person had a right to talk on the phone while driving and that it did not have to affect me unless I allowed it to. After this attitude adjustment I encountered increasingly fewer instances of oblivious drivers using mobile phones, and soon it was no longer a problem.

Could my attitude shift have affected the number of people who chose to use mobile phones while driving, or did it cause people to drive more skillfully while talking on the phone? Of course not! I create my own reality, not that of other people. Shifting my attention (and not focusing on my belief that talking on the phone while driving was irresponsible) resulted in a change in the type of experiences I drew to myself. It works this way with everything, which is why prejudice against a certain category of people can be so insidious. Someone with negative beliefs about a particular group tends to attract a disproportionate number of people from that group who fulfill her pessimistic expectations. These experiences serve to strengthen the belief, and it becomes a vicious circle.

The second example of how moving one's attention can result in tangible changes involves a plant. In the springtime my housemate and I bought a beautiful bright pink bougainvillea that graced our backyard all summer. These plants do not take well to extreme cold, so when fall arrived we moved the bougainvillea indoors. Right away I noticed that it dropped a large quantity of leaves and petals onto the carpet, to the point that I would barely finish cleaning up one batch before more would appear. The bougainvillea's constant defoliating became an annoyance, and I wondered if it had been a mistake to buy the plant. Its shedding of leaves and petals seemed to increase every week. One day, after picking up a plethora leaves and petals from the carpet, I looked – really looked – at the plant instead of at the carpet beneath it. The bougainvillea was bursting with gorgeous pink blossoms! For weeks I had noticed only the dead leaves and petals and failed to look at the plant itself. For the next few minutes I appreciated the splendor it offered, apologizing to the bougainvillea for having ignored it for so long. "With your beauty," I told the plant, "it's okay with me if you drop as many leaves and petals as you want."

Later that day I walked by the bougainvillea again. Typically it would have dropped at least a dozen leaves and petals in the amount of time since my last cleanup, but it had not lost a single one! In the following days I noticed that the plant's defoliating decreased markedly. It was not just my imagination; my housemate commented on the change as well. I did not move the bougainvillea, alter its watering schedule, or do anything other than switch my attention from the dropped leaves and petals to the plant itself. When I paid attention to the dead foliage, I got more dead foliage. When I shifted my attention to the beauty of the plant, I got more beauty, and the bougainvillea thrived. (Think about that the next time you start counting gray hairs!) This experience can serve as a metaphor for what many of us do habitually: we pay attention to things that annoy us and put a lot of effort into dealing with them. The solution is not to spend more time and effort "cleaning up dead leaves." All we need to do is to move our attention from what we don't want to what we do want.

How Creation Works

A significant distortion I have found in many spiritual teachings is the idea that we create our reality with our thoughts. This can be a difficult concept to comprehend, but thought is a mechanism of translation, not creation. What you think about often is what you create, but you do not have to think about something to create it. Several people have told me they gave no thought to aging until the day they looked in the mirror and noticed signs of it. Clearly they were influenced by the beliefs they held even though they did not translate these influences into thoughts.

We create through our perception, and what we create is molded by our beliefs. When we pay attention to feelings and other communications, the thoughts we generate can give us a big clue regarding the beliefs we hold and the experiences we are creating. Once we have that awareness, we can more consciously make choices that support our desires. Yet often we ignore communications from our inner self, try to override them with thoughts, and then wonder why we are not getting what we think we want.

We create our reality internally and project it outwardly, which is what forms our external world. Most of us tend to focus on the external reality almost exclusively. It is as if we are looking in a mirror observing the reflection of ourselves and what we are generating, but we are paying attention only to the reflection and forgetting what – and who – is creating it. It is analogous to a man looking in the mirror and noticing that his hair is in an unflattering style, his face is covered with stubble, and his shirt is askew. Rather than changing his hairstyle, shaving his face, and straightening his shirt, he tries to alter the reflection by force of will. He has an idea of the improvements he would like to make, but instead of taking action that would change himself (and alter the image he is projecting), he focuses positive energy at his reflection and appeals to deities for help in altering it. Of course, nothing really changes.

The key to conscious creation is recognizing the correlation between your inner world (your beliefs, choices, feelings, and habits) and the outer world (what you are experiencing). Once you understand how you are creating your world, you have the option to make choices that will manifest different results. It is as simple – and as challenging – as that.

Many of us tend not to pay attention to the feelings, thoughts, and beliefs that reveal what we are creating internally. Instead we scramble around, engaging in actions that fail to move us in the direction we want to go. I have noticed that when I easily create something I want, often I didn't really do anything but get out of my own way. In many cases, if I had stopped to ponder the matter, I probably would have short-circuited what turned out to be an effortless creation. The key to effective, purposeful creating is simply to allow it to happen rather than analyzing the things we are doing wrong and trying to correct them.

Another ineffective strategy (or lack of strategy) is idly waiting for something to happen, which seems to be the bane of many spiritually oriented people. It is more productive to focus on ideas and formulate them into tangible creations rather than passively waiting for something miraculous to fall out of the sky. When we have an intention and truly expect it to be fulfilled, it usually is. Expecting your desire to be fulfilled, however, does not necessarily mean you won't have to take action. At times you will be inspired to take action; follow these impulses even if they don't seem to make sense at first. Often you will find that things fall into place without any great effort or frenetic activity on your part.

When clarifying general intentions (such as those related to improvements in health or appearance), it is unwise to set deadlines for their manifestation. The concept of a *deadline* is limiting; the word itself has negative connotations. The term *goal* is more positive but still connotes completion at a certain point, which is not always appropriate. *Focus area* is the expression I like best.

People excel in the areas where they focus their attention and energy. Individuals who are outstanding in a particular field tend to be those who concentrate their energy most intensely on that subject or activity. This is true not only of geniuses, but of so-called idiot savants – they tune out distractions and focus with acute intensity on the task at hand. Our culture teaches us to scatter our energies, provides constant distractions, and places a high value on multitasking. Many of us lose touch at an early age with our inherent ability to concentrate our attention.

Impediments to Creation

In theory, to have what we want, we simply need to make a choice, set an intention, and allow it to manifest. In practice, this often is not as easy as it sounds. In Jane Roberts's book, *The Nature of Personal Reality*, Seth (the famous nonphysical personality) stated, "You get what you concentrate upon. There is no other main rule."[15] Many people have misinterpreted this statement to mean you get what you think about, which is not necessarily the case. Concentration involves your beliefs, intentions, and focus of energy, not simply your thoughts.

In some self-help methods, people are told that their thoughts create their reality, so they start forcing themselves to think positive thoughts (which in many cases directly contradict their beliefs) and judging themselves and others for thinking or saying anything "negative." But unless the positive thoughts are in alignment with the person's beliefs, this method of creating is ineffective. It is simply another way of trying to force "outer" reality to conform to what we want, without having any real understanding of the subjective aspect of creation.

When you are having trouble manifesting something you desperately want, the best course of action may be to move your attention to anything *but* the thing you want. When you keep thinking that something must happen, remind yourself that things are unfolding in the most beneficial manner. From your current perspective it seems as if events need to occur in a certain way at a certain time, but if you could see the larger picture, you would understand that what you want right now would not be most beneficial for you.

The core issue here is self-trust. When I am feeling upset about the possibility of something happening or not happening, it helps to remember that I would not betray myself. If something I want does not occur the way I would like it to, I take it as evidence that what I thought I wanted was not the most beneficial outcome for me at that time. If it were, it would have happened! When I think about things in this way, it immediately dissipates the pressure I am feeling. And on many occasions, it turns out that what I wanted manifests fairly quickly. Following are common reasons we have difficulty manifesting our desires.

Indecision

In situations where you feel you cannot make a decision and are continually vacillating, your indecision stalls the creation process. Ensuring that you make the best choice is often less important than the action of making *some* choice. By making a choice, you put your energy fully behind that choice instead of dissipating it by pondering the various alternatives. If it turns out that the choice does not serve your intentions very well, you can make another choice in the future. We always have options, even if we don't recognize them immediately.

An example of the downside of indecision is an employee who is dissatisfied with her job and cannot decide whether to stay or find a new one. Due to her uncertainty, she is not fully present in the job and does not perform as well as she could. Her halfhearted attempts at looking for other employment opportunities also fail to yield substantial results. In cases like this, what often happens is that eventually an (apparently) external event forces the person into action. The company reorganizes or downsizes, and the employee (who probably was not one of the top performers) is let go. Eventually she will find another job, but it would have been more advantageous for her to look for new employment on her own schedule, before she really needed it. If she had made the decision to stay in her current job, her performance probably would have been better and the company might have retained her.

At times when you feel you cannot make a decision or accomplish something you need to do, try substituting the word *won't* for *can't*. "I won't make a decision" has a different meaning from "I can't make a decision." When we say we won't do something, it connotes choice rather than inability. This simple change of semantics alters our perception and helps us recognize that the power is in our hands.

Another helpful approach is to substitute the word *choice* for *decision*. *Decision* is a serious word that connotes restriction and finality. *Choice* sounds more lighthearted and appealing; it seems less permanent and more open to future possibilities. Think about the ways we typically use these words: we must decide which job to take or college to attend, while we choose a flavor of ice cream or the color of a new shirt.

Conflicting Beliefs

Our world is based upon beliefs, and virtually everything we consider a truth is actually a belief. Beliefs themselves are neither good nor bad, but a certain belief may be inappropriate for a particular individual. If you align with a belief or set of beliefs, you are bound by its rules and limitations. If you do not align with it, those rules do not affect you. It is as simple as that. The difficulty arises when we hold two or more beliefs that conflict with each other.

Regarding aging, our culture has two strong beliefs that are completely incompatible. The first is that youth is highly desirable and virtually any evidence of aging is undesirable. The second is that age-related degeneration is largely unavoidable. Obviously, a person who holds both of these beliefs will have problems! If you align with only one, you are far less likely to experience conflict about aging. Most of us align with both beliefs at least to some degree; therefore we experience conflict about growing older.

Anet Paulina

Some people choose not to align with the first belief (that youth is good and aging is bad). In what is often called "aging gracefully," they accept the changes they believe are an inevitable part of growing older – without feeling discontented and losing self-esteem. In this book, it is apparent that I am addressing the second belief (that age-related degeneration is unavoidable). Neither approach is superior; it is simply a preference.

However, many of our beliefs are so ingrained that they are transparent to us – we don't even realize they are beliefs. An effective way to recognize your beliefs is to make a point of noticing your automatic reactions, feelings, and thoughts. Behind each of these is a belief (often multiple beliefs). For at least one day, make note of every belief you recognize, and then identify those that conflict with another belief you hold. Here is a strategy for discerning and dealing with conflicting beliefs:

1) Notice your automatic reactions – how you feel and what you think, say, and do.

2) Identify the beliefs that motivate these reactions and choices.

3) Remind yourself that they are beliefs, not truths.

4) Recognize the areas where you have conflicting beliefs.

5) Offer yourself a choice as to which beliefs you want to align with.

Sometimes our beliefs about what we want are inconsistent with our beliefs about what is possible. If we do not believe it is probable (or even possible) that we can manifest something, it is unlikely that we will. Conscious creating is a continuum: doubt, hope, expectation, and certainty. The closer you are to certainty, the greater the likelihood that what you want will manifest. You can think positive thoughts until the cows come home, but the cows won't come home unless you truly believe they will.

Focusing on Lack

When we want something (health, a youthful appearance, money, or a harmonious relationship), often we focus more on the lack of it than on having it. We attract what we focus upon, so when we focus on lack, we create more lack. This is a common reason for not manifesting what we desire. Sick people who concentrate on their disease create more disease. Individuals who focus on their shortage of money continue to manifest a shortage. Those who have experienced trauma and keep thinking and/or talking about the experience (including in a support group setting) are likely to continue to feel the effects of the trauma. If they focus on it enough, they may attract similar experiences in the future.

Focusing on lack also can be done collectively, which often happens when there are drought conditions in an area. People start focusing on the lack of rain, so that is what they manifest: continued lack of rain. A more productive way to think about a drought is that it is similar to what happens when a person goes on a crash diet: he can maintain the restriction for a while, but eventually he binges. That is what a geographical area does when there is a drought: it goes on a moisture starvation diet but eventually reverts back to its natural state, which includes rain. Once the rain starts, it often rains a lot, much like a person who abandons a strict diet and goes on an eating spree. This is nature's way of maintaining balance.

Several years ago in the area where I lived, weather conditions had been unusually dry for a long time. A common topic of conversation was the drought and the dire consequences that could occur if it continued. Intending to do something constructive about the situation, several friends and I pooled our energies. We stated our intention for rain, visualizing and imagining what we would experience when it was raining. I thought of rainy spring and summer days when I was a child – how the rain felt and smelled, what it looked and sounded like, and the fun I had playing in the mud puddles afterward. Other group members started expressing what it was like for them during a rain shower. Two days later, it rained for the first time in weeks – a steady, soaking rain that lasted for hours. Over the next few days it rained periodically, and soon it was apparent that the drought had ended.

Frequently giving attention to something you do not prefer is analogous to continually snacking on candy and wondering why you are overweight! Unfortunately, most of us have been taught to solve problems by focusing on them (the conventional medical system is based on this premise), and learning to do otherwise can seem daunting.

To change the habit of focusing on problems, you must first be aware that you are doing it. To catch yourself when you start concentrating on something negative, notice your feelings, thoughts, words, and actions. If you find it difficult to keep your attention on a positive outcome (health instead of illness, for example), switch focus and change the subject completely. Stop thinking about health or finances and start thinking about your favorite vacation area or your cat. Play some music that will lift your mood, start reading that new novel, or initiate a game of hide-and-seek with your kids. Improving your mood and attitude makes a difference in the type of experiences you attract, including those that seem completely beyond your control. Even if it has no discernible effect on your experiences, at least you will feel better.

Attachment to the Outcome

The key to manifesting our desires is attention without attachment. Think of a beam lying on the floor. If you wanted to walk across the length of the beam without falling, you probably could do so without much difficulty. Now visualize the same beam suspended above a 50-meter chasm. Could you walk across the beam with the same ease you did before? Probably not. Yet it is the same beam, so what is the difference? The difference is *attachment to the outcome.* When the beam was on the floor, you were willing to walk across it and accept the outcome whether you stayed on or fell off. With the beam placed higher, however, you would be unwilling to accept the outcome of falling, which likely would result in serious injury or death.

It is the same with most things in life: if we are not attached to the outcome, we can accomplish our goals almost effortlessly. It is our attachment to the outcome that causes us to contract in fear and restrict the natural flow that allows us to fulfill our intentions with ease. When I had job interviews, for instance, I noticed that if I strongly wanted a particular position, usually I would not receive an offer. Yet if I had a "take it or leave it" attitude about the job, the employer often did make an offer. When I desperately wanted the position, my attachment to the outcome short-circuited its manifestation.

Flexibility (not being attached to a specific result) also is helpful in conscious creation. As long as it does not conflict with your life intentions, you can have virtually anything you want if you are flexible about how it manifests. For example, a person who needs a reliable car but lacks the financial resources to buy one should not limit himself to wanting only a vehicle of a particular make, model, color, and year. It may turn out that a friend is planning to trade in her stylish, well-maintained car for another vehicle and would be happy to sell the car for a modest sum. When specifying your desires, it helps to be as flexible as possible while still being satisfied with the potential result.

There is another school of thought that says it is easier to manifest something specific because you have precisely defined what you want. I have seen this method work as well. The approach that is likely to be more effective for you depends on your beliefs and the influences you are choosing in that particular circumstance. Once again, there are no absolutes.

Perfectionism

If you are trying to be perfect, your fear of making mistakes can inhibit your desire to take action, leading to a state of inertia and stagnation. Striving for perfection also results in inflexibility and an unwillingness to try new things. "Mistakes" are simply learning experiences we choose to label in a negative way. Rather than striving for perfection, aim for improvement. Perfection is a paradox: nothing is ever really perfect, yet everything is perfect just as it is. Perfection implies completeness, and everything is in a continuous state of becoming. In the objective sense, perfection is an unreachable goal. Do the best you can and just go with it. Even the result does not seem to be quite what you had in mind, later it may turn out that you like the outcome better than the one you thought you wanted.

Although we characterize virtually everything as either good or bad, there really are no good or bad decisions; we just choose different experiences. The greatest regrets in life are not the things you have done that did not work out well – they are the things you wanted to do but lacked the courage, energy, or self-confidence to pursue.

Intentions Versus Wants

There is a difference between *intentions* and *wants*. We may want something, but if having it does not support our basic intentions (the life plan of our inner self), it is unlikely the desire will manifest. In cases where I seem to do everything right without success (and don't have conflicting beliefs blocking the manifestation), I usually conclude that what I want would not be appropriate for me at that time.

Most of us assume we are aware of our intentions, but this is not always the case. For instance, nearly everyone says they would like to win the lottery, but actually having it happen would be disturbing to most people. Their way of life would change abruptly – they would be forced out of their comfort zone and subjected to media attention and demands from family, friends, and strangers. They would have to decide how to invest and/or spend the money and might feel guilty for not using it to help those in need. The surefire way to avoid these pressures and choices is to *not* win the lottery – so most of us don't.

Resentment

When we have struggled with something and observe someone who achieved the same or better results without the struggle, it is natural to feel some resentment. Not only are we likely to envy the person, we also may feel their experience somehow invalidates our own achievement – or our pain. If we slaved for years to reach a goal and discover that another person reached or exceeded the same goal in less time and with less effort, we feel as if our time and effort were wasted. In fact, nothing was wasted; we chose those challenges for the value of the experiences, not just as a means to an end.

At times I've noticed that when I have something I think other people might envy, I tend to either discount it in some way or make a point of how hard I worked for it. Feeling I must justify my success or "good fortune" is aligning with limiting beliefs as well. Each of us has areas in which things come easily and other areas we find challenging. Rather than resenting those who find our difficult areas easy, we can consider them examples of what is possible. As long as we begrudge others having money, business success, good health, beauty, a fulfilling relationship, or anything else we covet, we won't be able to create it for ourselves. You cannot become what you resent.

Creating What You Want

Appreciation

Appreciation is one of the easiest and most effective ways to shift your energy quickly. Switching from focusing on problems (which tends to exacerbate them) to focusing on positive aspects of your life makes you feel better immediately and also attracts more such things. In addition, finding something to appreciate about circumstances and events that initially distressed you can be even more powerful.

To develop the habit of appreciation, play the "appreciation game" consistently for at least 30 days. Every day, make note (in a journal, electronic document, or with a voice recorder) of three things you appreciate. Be genuine (choose things that truly elicit a feeling of appreciation in you) and specific. Rather than saying, "I appreciate my friend Ava," you might say, "I appreciate Ava's dry wit and odd sense of humor." Make sure one of the three items is something you appreciate about yourself (a quality or accomplishment) and another item is something you appreciate about another person. Beyond that, anything goes. At the end of 30 days, it is likely you will notice you have drawn more things into your life that you appreciate.

Humor

If anything in our world comes close to being a panacea, it is humor and levity. People have used humor to cure themselves of supposedly incurable diseases. Being able to laugh about something and not take circumstances too seriously cuts the thickness of energy and relieves tense situations. There have been times when I have felt myself on a downward spiral, with one thing after another going wrong. The fastest and most effective way I have found to reverse that energy is to genuinely and heartily laugh.

Humor also can be the best defense. Rather than fighting against something that upsets you, try making fun of it. This is a great strategy for dealing with things that seem to be out of your control, such as political decisions. The idea of not fighting against circumstances and choosing to go with the flow of life is simple but profound. When I step back and view the world from a broader perspective, the struggling, forcing, and fighting we do seems silly. Most people take life far too seriously and need to lighten up. When we have moved on to other realms, the things we worry and obsess about won't really matter. Why not make the decision now to take life less seriously and appreciate the humor in daily events?

Manifesting Wealth

Money (or in New Age parlance, prosperity or abundance) is a subject intrinsically related to how we experience life. Like emotional baggage and physical clutter, financial worries can affect how a person experiences aging. Some of the most common limiting beliefs about money are that money is scarce and hard to acquire, having money is not spiritual, making a lot of money means you have "sold out," and wealth leads to unhappiness.

It is common for even middle-class people to have a poverty mentality. They have enough money to cover their basic expenses and are not in serious debt, yet they worry about every expenditure, hold on tightly to material things in general, and resent those who have more than they do. Because they restrict the natural flow of resources, their income is low. In contrast, people who have a wealth mentality tend to draw opportunities (and to recognize and act on these opportunities). Folks with a poverty mentality are less likely to attract opportunities and often don't take advantage of those that come their way.

People who worry about money a great deal and fret over virtually every expenditure typically have difficulty acquiring wealth. Often they work hard but have little to show for their efforts. I experienced this myself when I moved to a new city and had trouble getting a job. Concerned that I would run out of money, I became very thrifty and worried about even small purchases. And what did this frugality lead to? A job where I worked hard, contributed significantly to the company, and regularly participated in management meetings, yet was paid a low wage with no benefits. In sharp contrast are people who have the attitude that money is plentiful and easy to make. They don't become stressed about finances and seem to attract wealth almost effortlessly.

If we could think of money the way we think of air, we would not experience scarcity. Air is more essential to our physical survival than food, water, or anything money can buy. If deprived of oxygen for more than a few minutes, we perish. Yet most of us never worry about getting enough air. We have no doubt that the next time we need to take a breath, there will be plenty of oxygen, and there always is. If we had the limiting beliefs about air that most of us have about money, we would try to breathe in as much air as possible and retain it as long as we could. People would live in fear that there would not be enough air for everyone, resenting those who seemed to use more than their fair share of this invisible elixir. Hoarding air in storage tanks would be commonplace, and people would write their wills with a provision to leave the storage tanks to their loved ones. This scenario may sound ridiculous, but it is no more ridiculous than our insecurity about the availability of money or other resources. It is our belief in scarcity (based upon lack of self-trust) that creates conditions of insufficient resources.

When you feel enthusiastic about an idea, it is worthwhile to pursue it even if there do not seem to be immediate gains. Creating wealth and opportunities can be like turning on a faucet: you start out with a few drops that join to create a trickle before becoming a full stream. Don't give up too soon; allow the momentum to build.

Body Consciousness

One of the keys to establishing communication and cooperation with a life form is to recognize and appreciate its attributes. Our physical bodies are comprised of a variety of conscious "beings" such as organs and cells. Most of us take for granted the functions they perform, but if there is a problem, we resent the offending body part.

What if, instead of noticing only the things we dislike, we acknowledged some of the innumerable ways in which our bodies serve us well? For instance, rather than becoming angry with your skin over a pimple or rash, appreciate the beneficial things your skin does for you: it protects your body, insulates and cools you, allows you to feel the pleasure of touch, and gives you an attractive appearance. Feeling angry with your skin over a small problem is like being an unappreciative manager with an excellent employee. The employee does a superb job without needing supervision, yet the manager never notices. But if the employee does something the manager disapproves of, the manager reads him the riot act. The employee likely feels unappreciated and assumes the manager does not notice or care about his hard work. Lack of appreciation is one of the greatest causes of low motivation. Our cells generally continue to do their jobs no matter how badly we treat them, but I cannot help but think they would benefit from appreciation.

Developing communication and cooperation with all aspects of our body can facilitate its functioning and allow us to determine more easily the cause of any problems that occur. Instead of looking at yourself and noticing only what you think needs improvement, start focusing on traits you like. If you observe something that seems out of place, ask your body to let you know what the problem is and what you can do to help. Clear your mind and allow the communication to come through. Very likely (although perhaps not immediately), you will receive information that provides insight into the cause of the problem and what you can do to help your body restore its balance.

Manifesting Physical Changes

A man I know was distressed that he was losing his hair at a rapid rate and had been told that his type of hair loss did not respond well to oral or topical pharmaceutical treatments. His problem was interesting to me because it was analogous to challenges most of us have experienced with physical conditions and characteristics we want to change. It seems that the more we resist the unwanted manifestation, the worse it becomes. When pondering this man's difficulty, a thought entered my mind: *You must accept your creation before you can make another choice.* In devising a method to reach this state of acceptance, I came up with the following ideas.

The first step is to develop an attitude of feeling neutral about the condition or characteristic. You might not be happy about it, but you are not resisting it. When you truly are in a state of acceptance (nonresistance), you can choose to alter the physical manifestation – or not. The main challenge, of course, is how to arrive at this state of acceptance. When I was younger, I was very critical of many of my physical features. One thing that helped was noticing people I admired who had similar characteristics. Observing that a person I considered attractive possessed some of the same traits I did made it easier to accept those traits in myself.

For the man who was concerned about impending baldness, I suggested he talk with men who obviously had been bald for a long time and seemed comfortable with their appearance. It is likely they would remember how it felt when they started losing their hair, and they might be open to sharing their experiences and views with him. I also suggested he discuss the subject with female friends. When the topic has come up with women I know, most have said they find bald men as attractive as those with a full head of hair.

For the second step of the method (making another choice), it is necessary to believe you *can* make a different choice. It helps to read or hear accounts of people who have made drastic physical changes believed by medical science to be impossible. *The Holographic Universe* includes many such stories that are well documented. In one case, it shows the before-and-after x-rays of a man who regenerated his hipbone after it was destroyed by cancer.[16] If someone can grow a new hipbone, I told my friend, it shouldn't be too hard to grow hair! There are about 100,000 hair follicles on the scalp, many of which are dormant most of the time and can be activated.

Another key factor for manifesting physical changes is to stop paying attention to what you dislike. When we focus on something we don't like, we recreate it in every moment. To deal with hair loss, for example, stop paying attention to your receding hairline, how thin your hair is getting, and how many strands you are losing each day. When you look in the mirror, probably the first thing you notice is your hairline. Catch yourself having this automatic reaction and switch your focus to another feature, preferably one you like. At first you may have to force yourself to do this, but soon it will become a habit. If you notice a lot of hairs on your pillow or in your comb, remind yourself that they are old hairs being discarded to make way for new ones. Trust yourself to create what best serves your intentions.

Visualization

Visualization practices can be helpful for understanding the dynamics that are creating a physical condition as well as for making changes. The following visualization technique can be tailored to your preferences. When you are ready to begin your visualization, if you are not already in a positive, optimistic mood, do whatever will help you reach this state. Relax your body and clear your mind. It helps to spend a few minutes in a meditative state before starting the visualization.

Visualization includes not just mental images (which some people find difficult to create), but feelings, sensations, sounds, and scents. As much as possible, imagine yourself truly experiencing what you want your future to be like. It is essential to make this state feel authentic, so you may want to start small. For instance, if you have a long-term weight problem, you may not yet be able to envision yourself as very slender, but you probably can imagine comfortably wearing clothes a few sizes smaller than you wear now. Continue your visualization only as long as it holds your interest (probably five minutes at most). If you start having contradictory feelings or thoughts ("I could never look that way"), it is time to end the exercise. The images and feelings you generate in the visualization are themselves a creation, one you can tap into at any time. Even momentary flashes of your inner creation help it manifest physically.

A different type of visualization can be used to create a specific bodily condition. This method is particularly effective with health and appearance-related concerns. Here is an example of using this type of visualization to stimulate hair growth: Imagine a field of wheat in which some of the plants are green and supple, while others are old and dry (coarse, gray hairs). Perhaps the ground (scalp) is dry and cracked; there may be bare (bald) patches where no plants are growing. Imagine the ground becoming hydrated (improved circulation), new plants sprouting in the bare patches, and old stalks becoming green and supple (coarse, gray hairs regaining their original color and texture). Once you have developed this visualization, you can refer to it whenever you think of your hair and scalp, reminding yourself of the changes being made.

Chapter 5

Emotional Clearing

~~~

Paradise is there, behind that door, in the next room, but I have lost the key. Perhaps I have only mislaid it.

—Kahlil Gibran (Lebanese-American writer, 1883–1931)

Self-Acceptance

Lack of self-acceptance (along with its companion, lack of self-trust) is fundamental to most of the problems we experience. Paradoxically, accepting ourselves as we are now (not as we expect to be after we have increased our income, lost weight, or met the right partner) not only allows us to be happier in the moment, it helps attract the things we desire. If we feel we won't be "good enough" until we have these things, then we probably don't feel good enough to deserve them. It can become a vicious circle that leaves us chronically dissatisfied.

Humans have a basic need to acknowledge, accept, fully integrate, and share with significant others the fundamental aspects of their personality. Keeping them hidden is the psychological equivalent of imprisoning an objectionable family member in the basement. Unfortunately, by the time we reach adulthood, most of us have come to believe we are inferior or deficient in some manner.

It is easy to understand how those with major physical or mental challenges could feel this way; it can be difficult to maintain self-esteem when immersed in a culture with belief systems that assess a person's worth based on arbitrary standards you know you don't match. Yet haven't you ever looked at yourself as objectively as possible and concluded that you must be nuts to be so full of self-doubt? It's the feeling you have when you are walking down the street, feeling inadequate because you gained a little weight, received a B instead of an A on a test, or didn't make that tough sale. Then you see a disabled person who has to put forth major effort just to propel himself a short distance down the street. In truth, what do most of us have to complain about? I sometimes imagine us after we have passed on from this world, looking back on our lives and feeling like fools because we wasted so much time and energy worrying about what was "wrong" with us.

Mirroring

Everything in our outside environment is a manifestation of what is inside us. If we fail to recognize our own characteristics, we may see them reflected in the people and events around us, sometimes in an exaggerated fashion. The reflection is not always direct, however. Encountering an angry person, for instance, does not necessarily mean you have anger issues. It may indicate that you are intolerant or afraid of people who seem angry or out of control, or that you are restricting some other type of energy that needs to be expressed.

The mirroring concept also applies in *feng shui* (the Chinese art of placement) and *vastu shastra* (the Hindu system of architectural design that likely was its predecessor). When a person has problems with finances, for example, it is not because the prosperity areas in his home are poorly arranged. Actually the reverse is true: the arrangement of the prosperity areas reflects the way he handles finances. People design their environments in ways that mirror their beliefs, and the environments reinforce those beliefs. Feng shui and vastu shastra techniques often work because the person recognizes his beliefs and alters his physical surroundings to reflect his new attitude. The external changes may help him avoid reverting back to old patterns. It also is possible to jumpstart inner changes by making physical alterations. Cleaning out a closet can lead to seemingly unrelated life changes.

Judgment and Negativity

The term *judgment* often is used to mean *nonacceptance*: the belief that something should be different from the way it is. In truth, right and wrong are simply a matter of perspective. Virtually everyone acts from what they perceive are good intentions, regardless of how terrible you may view their actions to be. The key element here is perception, and one person's perception may be radically different from another's. Judgment is a natural product of holding beliefs, and beliefs are inherent to our world. Telling yourself not to judge is like telling yourself not to breathe – it is only a matter of time until you cannot help but do it again. Judgment also involves choice, and it is important to distinguish between making choices for you (which is necessary and appropriate) and making choices for other people, which in most cases is inappropriate. When making choices for yourself, think of it as discernment or evaluation rather than rather than judgment, which almost by definition incorporates negativity.

To minimize the time and energy you spend judging other people, develop the habit of remaining neutral rather than automatically labeling things as positive or negative. Neutrality in this context means detachment, which is not the same as indifference. Indifference indicates a lack of caring, but you can be neutral and still feel concerned. When you cannot help but lapse into judgment, try to observe your reactions in a detached way, without attempting to suppress or intensify them.

Triple-A Process

If you are having negative feelings about something, try using my three step Triple-A process (Acknowledge, Address, and Abandon):

1) *Acknowledge* what you are feeling; don't try to rationalize or deny it. Emotions are a form of communication. Overriding emotions with thoughts is like pushing a floating cork under the water: it is only a matter of time before it pops up again.

2) *Address* the issue or concern as best you can. Addressing the issue may involve taking action or venting your frustration by writing about it or engaging in physical activity. If you cannot come up with an appropriate action, you may be able to address the issue by altering the way you view it.

3) *Abandon* your thoughts about the issue – let it go and don't keep dwelling on it. At this point (in contradiction to the earlier example), you may have to push the cork down a few times until it remains submerged. If you still continue thinking about the issue, it is likely you have not adequately addressed it.

Managing Negativity

An even simpler technique for dealing with negativity is to assess honestly what benefit there is to having the negative thoughts and judgments. What is the worst that could happen if you did not have these thoughts? Is there a constructive action you could take that you have not taken already? Imagine how you would feel if you ceased having the negative thoughts and judgments – would you feel better or worse than you do now?

Consider how differently you might treat other people (and yourself) if you were not judging them or you. If your imagined scenario seems like a happier one (and it almost always does), you may find yourself choosing that alternative rather than continuing on your current track. When judgments and negative thoughts are reframed as a conscious choice, it becomes obvious that the best alternative is the one that feels better.

Attaining Acceptance

What Is Acceptance?

Dictionary definitions of acceptance include "favorable reception; approval, belief in something; and agreement." I interpret the concept of acceptance in a broader sense, as the action of perceiving something without believing it needs to change or be changed. A crucial point about the broader view of acceptance is that accepting something does not mean you must like it. Regardless of how much you may detest something, you acknowledge that it has the right to be the way it is. In the nonacceptance type of judgment, you believe it needs to change. Here is a helpful way I've found to view things: I do not have to like it, support it, want to interact with it, or participate in it in any way – but it (whatever "it" may be) has the right to exist, just as it is.

Lack of acceptance of people, situations, events, or anything else almost always stems from lack of acceptance of self. A person who truly accepts himself reflects acceptance to everyone. Being in his presence is like standing in front of a mirror that always makes you look magnificent. Others love to be around such a person because it feels wonderful to bask in the glow of total acceptance, to gaze into a mirror that makes you look so exquisite.

Judging yourself for doing something wrong is a form of nonacceptance. There are many experiences I would not want to repeat, but that doesn't mean it was wrong to have had them. I can choose to something different the next time without discounting myself for what I have chosen in the past. My previous creation was just the way it should have been, and now I am creating something different, which also will turn out appropriately.

Acceptance and Aging

In addition to understanding that age-related degeneration is not inevitable, an essential key to the aging dilemma is to accept what you have created. Acknowledge, without judgment, the health or appearance changes that are physical manifestations of a belief in degeneration. Acceptance does not mean you have to like these conditions, nor does it mean you cannot change them. When we accept what we have created, it frees us to create differently in the future. The key is noticing without judging.

Paradoxically, truly accepting what you have created allows you to make a different choice. It is acceptable to use health therapies, cosmetic treatments, or other physical means of improving the functioning or appearance of something you do not prefer. Knowing you have these options can make it easier to accept a condition you find uncomfortable or unappealing. It is quite possible, however, to alter these conditions without using physical methods. (Notice I used the term *condition* rather than *feature* or *characteristic*, which imply permanence.)

The concept of acceptance is paradoxical, which makes it difficult to explain logically. Accepting a condition does not mean you will be stuck with it for life. On the contrary, it gives you the freedom to make another choice. However, trying to accept something only because you want to change it is not true acceptance; it is just fooling yourself. True acceptance entails feeling at peace with whatever you create: stiff joints or flexibility, baldness or a full head of hair, a slim figure or a portly one. Admittedly, this is much easier said than done.

An additional challenge is that acceptance is not necessarily permanent. You may be in a state of acceptance today, but tomorrow you might wake up feeling troubled by the same issues. If this happens to you, do not despair. Every moment you spend in acceptance "counts" and makes it easier to sustain that state for longer periods. When I have reached a state of acceptance about aging issues, it has felt liberating.

When I started working on this book, the thought of speaking in public about aging made me apprehensive. Although I am deeply inspired to share my knowledge on this subject with others, I was concerned that I might be criticized for not looking like a 25-year-old. (The irony is that I didn't look 25 even when I was 25! From my twenties to mid-thirties, people typically thought I was at least five years older than my actual age.) Since I understand that age-related degeneration is due to beliefs, I judged myself harshly for having some physical signs of aging. After all, I "know better" and therefore should not be manifesting something I find undesirable.

Unfortunately, that is not quite the way it works. Understanding these concepts intellectually does not necessarily change one's beliefs, at least not right away. My current beliefs are such that I am confident about maintaining good health and optimum physical and mental functioning, but less certain that I can completely avoid various aesthetic aspects of aging. Finally I acknowledged that it is all right for me not to be perfect; it doesn't invalidate the truth of the concepts. Putting pressure on oneself to look younger (and being attached to the outcome) only makes it more difficult to transcend limiting beliefs about aging.

Accepting What Is

Since it affects everything in our lives, addressing the lack of acceptance (of both ourselves and others) is well worth the effort. The challenge, of course, is finding a way to reach a state of acceptance regarding something you dislike. When you make statements such as, "I weigh too much" or "I shouldn't have these lines under my eyes," question yourself. Why should or shouldn't you have the weight or wrinkles? The fact is that you do have them; there has no "should" about it. They are an aspect of you, something you have manifested. These conditions may not be what you prefer, but they are not intrinsically bad. Ask yourself what is really wrong with having them – does it make you an unworthy person? It is doubtful that you consider other people with a full figure or facial lines to be unworthy, so there is no reason to judge yourself that way. There is nothing inherently wrong with any physical condition. Allowing yourself permission to be the way you are is incredibly freeing.

Another helpful approach for accepting physical conditions is to remind yourself that most of them are (or can be) temporary rather than permanent. This applies not just to conditions commonly believed to be easily changeable (such as body weight and muscle tone), but also to facial lines, thinning hair, and most health problems. There is virtually nothing about ourselves that we cannot change. We create a "new" body in each moment; physical conditions appear permanent simply because we keep recreating them in the same way. When you notice something about yourself (aesthetic or functional) that you dislike, remind yourself that it is temporary condition you can change. I find it easier to accept something undesirable if I believe it isn't permanent.

I have adopted the attitude that things always work out for the best, even if it doesn't seem so at first. When I find myself worrying about something, I remind myself that however it works out ultimately will be most beneficial for me. This attitude eliminates much of the anxiety I used to feel about a variety of situations.

Clearing the Past

Unresolved emotional issues (often referred to as "emotional baggage") can cause a person to feel old, which leads to age-related degeneration. Many people associate their wrinkles and gray hair with difficulties they have experienced. They wear them almost as a badge of accomplishment, like a battle-scarred veteran proud of his war wounds. Others would very much like to unload their emotional baggage but fear they will be stuck with it for life. If this is the case with you, read on! There are methods that can help.

A persistent emotional issue such as long-term guilt or a traumatic memory is held in your energy field and body tissues, and it affects you much like chewing gum stuck to your shoe. It is a constant, low-level annoyance that keeps you from moving efficiently. The more you walk, the more junk gets stuck to the gum, until eventually it seriously impedes your progress. The obvious solution is to remove the gum and the attached debris. Sometimes you have to dislodge a lot of debris before you can even see the chewing gum (original problem) itself.

Many people talk about wanting to get rid of emotional baggage and memories that make them feel bad. It is not necessary to eradicate the memories themselves; the problem is the emotional charge associated with the memories. When we cease judging ourselves and others, that charge is neutralized. Emotional trauma is similar to allergies: it is not so much what happens, but one's reaction to what happens that causes the discomfort.

As best you can, jettison bad feelings about the past and wipe the slate clean of any resentment, bitterness, or grudges you are holding. Choose not to give attention to anything you have experienced that makes you feel bad when you think about it. There is no point in expending energy resenting what happened in the past, no matter how difficult or traumatic it was. The energy you put into resentment and rumination about past injustices not only fails to help you resolve the issues; it may draw more such experiences to you. It can be helpful to know what our fears and insecurities stem from, but it is not necessary to keep recreating them in the present.

Speaking from experience, I can assert that this is much easier said than done! Like many general principles, it falls into the category of "simple but not easy." Knowing we have a choice in the matter is helpful, however. Sometimes I find myself thinking about an unpleasant experience and realize that I am not quite ready to let it go. In some cases it has taken a few months before I reached a state of neutrality about something I experienced as very hurtful. But in such matters, months is preferable to years – or a lifetime. A troublesome situation that keeps coming up in your life may be resurfacing because you are not done with it energetically. One way of viewing things would be to say that your past issues and experiences are the problem. Because you have not resolved them, you are attracting similar circumstances into your life. However, it might be more accurate to view the experiences as facets of a theme you wanted to explore. A similar situation may be developing again so the theme can play out enough to lose its emotional charge.

Victim Mentality

"Victim mentality" is the belief that something can be foisted upon you by another person or an outside force – that something can happen to you without your having a choice in the matter. You always have a choice, although you may not be consciously aware that you chose a particular experience. How one reacts to the resulting situation is irrelevant. A person who fights back can have victim mentality just as much as one that withdraws and feels sorry for himself.

Rather than seeing myself as a helpless victim, I now view past traumas and dramas as if everyone simply played out their role, like in the theater. Some people play the part of the bad guy and others play the victim, but everyone involved has agreed to participate. Viewing experiences in this manner helps me maintain a more neutral, nonjudgmental mindset, removing the emotional charge from potentially distressing memories. At times I still feel like a victim, but now I acknowledge that I chose that role. This may seem oddly dichotomous, given our present mass belief systems, but in some cases I acknowledge that another person acted in an inappropriate manner and that I (for my own reasons) chose to participate in the scenario. This does not excuse the other person's behavior, nor does it invalidate the pain I experienced. It does, however, place the situation in a broader perspective.

Shifting Attention

An alternative to working through emotional issues is to shift your attention and choose to focus on something else. If you truly can do this, it is the most efficient method for dealing with depressing thoughts and troubling memories. Shifting your attention is not the same as "burying" feelings, although these actions can appear the same on the surface.

If you cannot genuinely shift your attention, it usually is better to examine and work through the feelings rather than trying to ignore them. Almost inevitably, they will surface later in some other form (possibly illness, depression, or anger over another issue). When you have negative feelings about something, forcing yourself to focus only on the positive aspects is a form of resistance – you are denying and resisting what *is*. Instead, acknowledge that you created the situation, feel the negative emotions, and let them flow through you.

I discovered that when I am feeling worried or hopeless, if I deliberately take an action that diverts my attention to something other than what is troubling me, I feel better almost immediately. This idea may not seem profound, but for me it was. It is analogous to falling into a ditch and choosing to crawl out of it rather than lying in the muck for days! Many people do this automatically, but I had to train myself.

A self-help technique called The Work® can be applied to virtually anything that troubles a person. The Work is a process of inquiry that teaches people to identify and question thoughts that cause suffering and to address their problems with clarity. Essentially, it is a way to reach a state of acceptance about things that it seems you cannot do much to change. The method was developed by Byron Katie, author of *Loving What Is: Four Questions That Can Change Your Life.*[17] Instructions and other pertinent information are available on her website (thework.com).

According to Katie, what makes people miserable is not the things that happen, but their thoughts about these events. Her method directly addresses troubling thoughts. Having seen Byron Katie in person and watched her help several audience members reach a state of acceptance about issues that had distressed them for years, I can affirm that her method can be broadly applied and highly effective. I have found that when I follow the process thoroughly and honestly, it yields results.

If you notice that the same types of issues and situations keep surfacing in your life, it is helpful to identify the underlying themes and core issues. Once you identify the themes, you can figure out the dynamics behind them – what the themes reveal about you. When you understand the basis of the issues, the energy behind them dissipates and you no longer continue to attract the same type of situations.

When you think of the past, remind yourself that those conditions and events exist only in your mind (and in the minds of others by mutual agreement). And you can change your mind in an instant.

Resistance to Change

When people have long-term physical, emotional, or financial problems, their ego tends to incorporate the characteristic as part of itself, almost like a limb or organ. The ego then fights to keep the problem, no matter how miserable it is making the person. If the individual's self-image doesn't change, the problem will remain, regardless of any treatment he receives. If a treatment is likely to work, he may reject it out of hand.

Sometimes the ego-self needs to be treated like a fearful dog that becomes aggressive when it senses a threat. It is only trying to protect you, but often it perceives danger where none exists. The dog needs to be gently led; trying to force it only makes things worse. Sometimes I feel like telling my ego-self to go sit in a corner and chew on a bone, but (like most dogs) it does not like being ignored and barks until I pay attention to it.

It is helpful to evaluate your motives on a regular basis. Are you doing – or not doing – something out of fear (the need to avoid a negative consequence) or joy (the desire to manifest something positive)? If acting out of fear, ask yourself what is the worst that is likely to happen if you adopt a more positive approach. If you think you can handle the least desirable possibility, consider switching from the fear-based course.

Spontaneous Change

Spontaneous remissions can occur with emotional problems as well as physical ones. This happened to me years ago when my almost lifelong fear of dogs simply vanished. Starting at age three when a collie jumped on me, I had a fear of dogs, especially large ones. I grew up in a rural area where dogs were allowed to run loose. Many times I was threatened or chased by a dog, and once I was bitten. Although it was not a serious injury, the experience was frightening. Whenever a large or rambunctious canine came near me, I felt uncomfortable or downright afraid.

As an adult I was employed in a building that occasionally was surveyed by security guards with drug-detecting dogs. One day I noticed a guard accompanied by a beautiful German shepherd. Rather than feeling wary of the creature, I was surprised to find I had a strong desire to pet it! I briefly considered asking the man if I could pet his canine assistant, but knew that working dogs are not supposed to be treated like pets when they are on the job. I was mystified by my uncharacteristic reaction, and later was even more surprised to discover it was not just a one-time occurrence. My fear of dogs had simply vanished!

After this incident I adopted a German shepherd puppy and developed a fondness for him that extended to other canines as well. Eventually I "adopted" a wolf I visited every few months. Usually he would be with several other wolves (all were socialized to humans), and their preferred method of greeting people was to jump up, place their forepaws on the person's shoulders, and lick their face. Here I was – a person who for most of her life had been afraid of large dogs that might jump on her – intentionally entering an area where wolves were jumping on her! I still have a healthy fear of canines that act threatening, but the inappropriate fear I experienced for so many years is completely gone.

I wish I could say precisely how I overcame my fear of dogs and provide five easy steps for eliminating fears and phobias, but I don't really know what caused this significant change. I did not undergo therapy, nor did I have a positive experience with a dog that might have changed my attitude. Without my conscious awareness, something within me shifted markedly. The point of relating this story is to demonstrate that this type of change can occur effortlessly.

Energy Psychology

Paying attention to what we are thinking enables us to become aware of thoughts that lead to stress and unhappiness, but most of us have automatic reactions that bypass the mechanism of thought. A person with a phobia of thunderstorms, for example, may hear a loud thunderclap and immediately feel fear. Much like the reflex of moving one's hand away from a hot surface, we react to certain stimuli without engaging a thought process.

Energy psychology techniques can be especially effective with these kinds of automatic reactions. They can eliminate (or at least diminish to manageable levels) emotional problems such as anxiety, fears, phobias, trauma, grief, guilt, anger, shame, and addictive cravings. The methods also have been successful with physical problems including headaches, body pains, breathing difficulties, and allergies. With energy psychology, these seemingly intractable difficulties may be eliminated or reduced in severity (sometimes in as little as a few minutes) by following simple procedures. The techniques are noninvasive and inexpensive, and you can perform most of them yourself. Visiting a practitioner for short-term treatment is considerably less costly (and in many cases, faster and more effective) than most forms of psychological therapy. There are books and videos that provide detailed information on various energy psychology techniques; instructions for some methods are available for free on the Internet.

Energy psychology is based on the premise that emotional (as well as physical) problems are characterized by disruptions in the body's energy field and that these issues can be treated with methods that affect the energy field. Proponents of energy psychology do not claim the techniques work for everyone, but many people have used them with excellent results. The procedures can be effective in a single session, but often multiple sessions are needed.

Most of the techniques can be performed alone or with the help of a friend, but there can be great value in consulting a skilled practitioner. The key to effectiveness is accurately identifying the issues to be treated, and core issues are not always apparent. Emotional problems can be like an onion, with numerous layers that must be peeled away before you reach the core. A practitioner can help identify these issues as well as provide instructions for correct use of the procedures. When people try one of the methods on their own without success, they may give up on energy psychology entirely and miss out on this valuable resource.

Critics of energy psychology claim there is no scientific basis for this type of therapy and that it works only because the patient believes it will work. In truth, all therapies (including conventional medical treatments) are based upon belief systems, and energy psychology is no exception. The lack of an explanation for how something works does not invalidate its effectiveness. Numerous pharmaceutical drugs have been effective despite the fact that when they were developed, scientists could not explain how or why they worked.

A possible explanation for the effectiveness of techniques involving the acupuncture meridians is that there is a crystalline matrix present in the connective tissue throughout the body that is piezoelectric (produces voltage when mechanical pressure or sound vibrations are applied). Acupuncture and acupressure techniques (including the acupressure holds and tapping procedures used in energy psychology) may work by sending piezoelectric impulses that are carried through the crystalline matrix in the connective tissue.

Some energy psychology methods involve the use of affirmations, which I generally do not recommend by themselves. Although affirmations sound good in theory (no pun intended), typically all you are doing is reminding yourself of – and reinforcing – what you truly believe, which usually is the opposite of the affirmation. However, when incorporated into energy psychology, hypnosis, and other types of altered-state mental programming, affirmations can be useful.

Energy psychology is a rapidly evolving field; numerous techniques are available and more are being developed. Regarding the effectiveness of various methods, there are no absolutes – virtually every method works for somebody, but no method works for everybody. Among the earliest methods discovered are those collectively known as thought field therapy, a term coined by Roger Callahan, PhD, who first developed the technique. With these methods, energy field disruptions can be corrected by tapping on acupressure points while the person being worked on "tunes in" to the problem being addressed.

Although in this book I cover energy psychology methods separately from "physical" energy healing methods, it is becoming apparent that the line between the two is blurring and likely will disappear. Ultimately all these methods may be most accurately described by the term *transformation*.

Emotional Freedom Techniques (EFT)

A widely used form of thought field therapy is EFT, a method developed by Gary Craig. The EFT website (emofree.com) offers a wealth of information, including specific instructions for performing the techniques. It also includes links to websites on other energy psychology methods. The EFT postal address is PO Box 269, Coulterville, California 95311 USA.

Not long after I learned about EFT, I was visiting a friend's family and had the opportunity to use the method with Sara, a woman in her thirties who had been afraid of dogs since she was bitten by one as a child. A few months before our visit, her husband had adopted a friendly and energetic Labrador retriever. Sara felt nervous around the dog and at one point had given her spouse an ultimatum: "It's either me or the dog." Things improved after the Lab went through obedience training, but the situation still was tenuous. It was apparent that Sara's husband dearly loved his canine friend; it would have broken his heart to give him up.

The night before I left, I told Sara about EFT and offered to download and print the EFT manual for her. Although she found the whole thing a bit odd, she was open-minded and motivated enough to try anything that might help. We printed the manual, read the most pertinent sections, and performed the procedure one time. The next morning Sara and I went through the tapping sequences again, this time with her husband watching. (From the look on his face, I was sure he must think I was a nut case but was too polite to say so!) It was several months before I received feedback on the effectiveness of Sara's EFT treatment. In a phone conversation with my friend, Sara's husband mentioned that her fear of dogs seemed to have disappeared. The last I heard, the family had adopted a miniature poodle because Sara wanted a dog of her own.

While EFT has significantly helped many people, it is not necessarily the most effective energy psychology technique for all individuals. You may find that another modality works as well or better for you. Following are brief descriptions of two other methods.

PSYCH-K®

PSYCH-K is an energy psychology therapy developed by psychotherapist Robert M. Williams, MA, after several years of research and working with thousands of individuals and groups. The method is believed to increase communication between the brain hemispheres and facilitate direct communication with the subconscious mind, enabling people to alter their beliefs and maximize their potential. PSYCH-K uses muscle testing and other techniques to identify beliefs and access the subconscious mind to achieve desired changes. It can be used to make changes in a broad range of areas including self-esteem, relationships, health, body image, prosperity, personal power, grief, and loss. For more information on PSYCH-K, see Rob Williams's website (psych-k.com) or contact the PSYCH-K Centre by phone at 800-567-3965 (toll-free).

Tapas Acupressure Technique® (TAT®)

TAT is an energy psychology therapy based on traditional Chinese medicine and yoga. Developed by acupuncturist Tapas Fleming, LAc, TAT involves placing one's attention on an issue while touching a few specific acupressure points on the face and back of the head. It is used for ending stress (especially traumatic stress) and allergic reactions; gaining self-confidence and a positive outlook on life; and attaining empowerment. For more information on TAT, refer to Tapas Fleming's website (tatlife.com) or contact TATLife by phone at 310-378-7381 or 877-674-4344 (toll-free).

Part Three:

Physical Strategies

Chapter 6

Health Without Hype

~~~

Preserving health by too severe a rule is a worrisome malady.
—Francois de La Rochefoucauld (French writer, 1613–1680)

Responsibility for Health

It amazes me that in the United States, people have given up primary responsibility for their health and placed it in the hands of the medical industry. Many health information sources incorporate warnings not to take virtually any health-related action without first checking with a doctor. The information purveyors do this to protect themselves from lawsuits, but it is unfortunate that such warnings have become a necessity. This mindset is so pervasive that it seems normal to most people. I sometimes wonder what will be next – recommendations that we consult a physician before taking a walk or eating a meal? The belief that we need direction and validation from some type of authority is widespread. I am amazed at the level of trust many people grant to an authority figure like a doctor, even if that person tells them to do something that defies both their instincts and common sense.

In my own version of a medical disclaimer, I would like to make it clear that in this chapter (and throughout the book) I am simply sharing my views, not telling readers how to live their lives. A fundamental concept of my philosophy is that each of us is responsible for our own well-being. If we choose to follow someone's advice (whether that person is a doctor, an author, or a stranger on the street), we are responsible for that decision. This idea flies in the face of the victim mentality so pervasive in our over-litigated society. Yet until we accept full responsibility for our bodies and our lives, we will continue to align with widely held beliefs that lead to poor health and age-related degeneration. It is crucial to recognize and heed your beliefs rather than ignoring or denying them. Some of the health-related ideas in this book may not be appropriate for certain individuals because they conflict with their present beliefs. As in all areas of your life, where health is concerned, follow your inner guidance.

As mentioned in the Preface, I intentionally chose not to provide scientific validation for all the health information in this book. Quantum mechanics (sometimes called quantum physics) proves that the observer affects what is observed, so there is no such thing as a truly "objective" study. Prevailing beliefs about what is beneficial or detrimental to our health shift radically from year to year. Substances as diverse as soybeans, coconut oil, eggs, potatoes, and coffee are demonized one year and exalted the next (or vice-versa). Where I present a product or practice as preferable to others, I note that the recommendation is based on a belief rather than an absolute truth. All such recommendations (regardless of the source) are based on beliefs. The crucial factor is whether you align with and choose to be influenced by those beliefs.

When something is found to have health benefits, it is touted as a panacea – until people start overdoing it and having bad reactions. The media loves to do this with many things including foods, nutritional supplements, and pharmaceutical drugs. First they go overboard reporting on how wonderful it is. When public interest wanes, they start disparaging the substance or practice and featuring articles about its dark side. The truth usually is somewhere in the middle.

Healthcare Services

There are many symptoms and conditions for which I would choose to seek medical treatment, but as a general rule I avoid doctor visits and diagnostic tests. When I used to go for checkups, I noticed that if I told the doctor I had no health concerns, he seemed a bit uneasy. It was apparent that he *wanted* to find something wrong! In an effort to please the physician, I would find myself trying to dredge up every health issue I had ever had. Afterward I would feel uncomfortable because I instinctively knew that focusing on past problems is counterproductive. The doctor's intention was not to cause me harm; according to his training and beliefs, there almost certainly was something wrong (or about to go wrong) with the health of a person over age 30. He simply wanted to find the problems and treat them to the best of his ability. Like virtually all medical doctors in our society, he was taught that disease and dysfunction are the norm and that a person in perfect health is an anomaly.

Putting myself in the place of a conventional physician who is introduced to unconventional health ideas, I can imagine how (as a writer) I would feel if someone invented a new language or discovered a method of communication that was more effective and efficient than writing in English. I have spent a great deal of time and effort honing my ability to write well in this language. It is a major area of expertise for me, something that makes me feel competent and useful. If English were scrapped in favor of a new language or communication method, the playing field would be leveled and I would lose my investment in this system. That must be how doctors and other experts feel when faced with new information that shifts the paradigm in their area of expertise. It is natural to be reluctant to give that up that investment, especially when you have incorporated those beliefs so deeply that they seem like truths.

Educational credentials show that a person has been programmed with the tenets of a particular belief system. A person with a medical degree has been programmed with conventional beliefs about health. Consider what someone must go through to become a physician: bombardment with information, lack of sleep, and unrelenting stress. The methods are similar to those used in brainwashing! In most information from medical doctors, I can discern a substructure of inflexible beliefs that likely were instilled during their training.

This is not to say I do not value the skills and contributions of medical professionals, nor am I opposed to consulting them. There have been times when I have felt that following the conventional medical route was the right thing to do; at other times I haven't. In an example of the latter, during a routine checkup in 1992 my doctor found what he thought were enlarged lymph nodes in my lower abdomen. Since I had no gynecological problems that might have affected nearby lymph nodes, he was almost certain this was an indication of non-Hodgkin's lymphoma (cancer of the lymphatic system) and directed me to have a biopsy.

The early symptoms of lymphoma are rather vague. While I had some of the symptoms (fatigue, chills, and itchy skin), they could just as easily have been due to working in a cold office in the wintertime in a job I disliked. I researched the disease and discovered that the recommended treatment was so harsh that it likely would have killed me before the cancer did. (I have severe reactions to virtually all medications that can cause nausea.) The biopsy would have damaged the lymph nodes even if they turned out to be healthy. Since I already knew I would not take the treatment, I saw no point in having a biopsy, so I refused it. Also, my gut feeling was that I did not have lymphoma.

To protect against a possible lawsuit, the doctor documented his preliminary diagnosis and recommendations and sent them to me in a letter. (Considering the number of lawsuits against medical professionals, I couldn't blame him.) The bottom line is that I never had the biopsy and am still very much alive and healthy. When I had another checkup two months later, the suspicious lumps were not there. Had I consented to the biopsy, my lymph nodes would have been damaged needlessly.

Diagnostic Tests

Despite the statistics that supposedly prove the value of various diagnostic tests, I choose not to subject myself to cholesterol screenings, mammograms, and other disease detection measures considered mandatory for health-conscious adults. If you search hard and often enough for something, it is likely you will create it eventually. It is normal for the human body to produce some irregular cells; most of the time it destroys them on its own.

I have long suspected that early detection methods for breast cancer are part of the reason the rate of this disease has skyrocketed. When a mammogram reveals a small cluster of "malignant" cells, doctors immediately take action with surgery, radiation, and/or chemotherapy. These assaults to the body weaken the immune system, allowing the cancer to take hold. If doctors had not interfered, the body might well have destroyed the abnormal cells on its own. The "cancer victim" would have remained healthy and been spared great physical, emotional, and financial trauma.

For a person with a fear of getting cancer and a strong belief in the conventional medical system, however, avoiding checkups probably would not be appropriate. It is imperative that you feel comfortable with the choices you are making. Not buying into the cancer industry in any manner makes me feel healthy and empowered, but if it would make you feel frightened and vulnerable, recognize and heed those feelings. If you believe you should have medical checkups, by all means do so. Nonetheless, it might serve you well not to completely dismiss the ideas presented here, which may prove helpful at some point.

An important caveat to my stance on avoiding routine doctor's visits and checkups is that I recognize there are times when the most appropriate way to address a health concern is to seek treatment from a medical doctor. Like most folks in modern society, I have a strong belief that medical treatment is necessary for many types of injuries and conditions. I have found that when I fight against my beliefs in any area (regardless of whether I like having those beliefs), the results are less than desirable. For example, in 2002 I developed symptoms of a kidney infection that did not respond to self-treatment with herbs. I resisted going to a doctor until I was in significant pain and continuously running a fever. Knowing that an untreated infection can cause permanent damage to the kidneys, I finally consulted a physician. The treatment turned out to be a five-day course of antibiotics that were inexpensive and caused no side effects. To unnecessarily risk kidney damage is sheer idiocy, and delaying medical treatment in this instance was very unwise.

Keep in mind that what you actually believe and what you *think* you believe may not be congruent. A woman I know, who earned an advanced degree in pharmacology but later became involved in holistic health care, thought she no longer aligned with beliefs about the need for conventional medical services. In less than a year she had two unexpected medical crises in which she was hospitalized. She did not have health insurance and ended up filing for bankruptcy because she could not pay her medical bills. I am sharing this story not to frighten you into buying health insurance, but to encourage you to be honest with yourself about your beliefs – as they are right now, not as you would like them to be.

Pharmaceutical Research

Beliefs are a fundamental factor in all research studies, and they affect study results to a far greater degree than is presently recognized. For instance, reliance on double blind, placebo-controlled studies in the pharmaceutical industry may have resulted in a preponderance of drugs that have more pronounced side effects than are necessary. Test subjects in these studies are not told whether the pills they are given contain a drug or an inert substance. If, however, the test subjects experience side effects, they can be reasonably certain they are receiving a drug rather than sugar pills. This knowledge strengthens their belief that the treatment will help their condition, making it more likely they will experience significant improvement.

Conversely, test subjects taking drugs with no discernible side effects have no evidence to indicate they actually are receiving a drug, so their belief in its effectiveness is not as strong. This difference in beliefs skews the study results so that drugs with strong side effects appear more effective than those with mild or no side effects. In the final stages of drug development, compounds with the most severe side effects (too harsh to be safely tolerated by most people) are eliminated from consideration, as are those with the least side effects (because they appear less effective than the other formulas). Compounds with moderate side effects usually are the winners, when in fact they may not be the most effective or the least harmful. This situation is just one example of the complex role beliefs play in health and healing.

Holistic and Conventional Medicine

Conventional Western medicine is excellent for treating traumatic injuries, cardiac arrest, acute infections, and other medical crises. I feel fortunate to have access to medical professionals and services that can handle these problems so effectively. When addressing chronic, long-term health issues, however, conventional medicine often falls short. The use of drugs and surgery for treating conditions like cardiovascular problems and cancer frequently leads to less-than-satisfactory results. The treatments themselves often cause additional health problems.

Holistic medicine emphasizes the importance of the whole and interdependence of its parts; the term is used to describe more natural alternatives to conventional medical therapies. Increasingly, the line of demarcation between the practice of conventional and holistic medicine is blurring. Chiropractors traditionally have had a holistic philosophy, but a growing number of conventionally trained medical doctors are becoming more holistic in their approach and more willing to use holistic therapies. Conversely, some "alternative" medicine practitioners are becoming less holistically oriented. This trend may be due to the requirements of managed-care insurance systems, many of which now cover some holistic therapies.

My contrasting experiences with acupuncturists illustrates how differently individuals can practice the same modality. In 1991 I had a series of acupuncture treatments from a doctor of Oriental medicine whose background included extensive training and experience in China. He focused not only on the problem I had consulted him for, but used a variety of diagnostic techniques (such as pulse and tongue analysis) to identify other imbalances.

When I consulted another acupuncturist in 2002, my experience was markedly different. This practitioner also was a doctor of Oriental medicine who had extensive training and experience in China. During the first visit, I was astonished when the doctor quickly scanned the forms I had filled out, asked me a few general questions, and immediately started treatment. Without so much as taking my pulse (an important diagnostic step that involves far more than the Western method of pulse taking), he had me lie down on the table, inserted a few needles, and scurried to the next treatment room. It seemed that his primary concern was to shuttle patients through his office as quickly as possible. In my view, this doctor was not practicing holistic medicine; he was practicing conventional medicine with needles!

A few weeks later I consulted a chiropractor about the same issues and was impressed with his thorough diagnostic approach, detailed explanations, and comprehensive treatment plan designed to achieve lasting improvements. The point I am making here is not that one type of treatment is superior to another; both acupuncture and chiropractic care (as well as most other modalities) can be effective when applied appropriately and correctly. My intention is to show that the healthcare world is changing so rapidly that it is best not to make blanket judgments about the value of one method over another. My disappointing experience with the second acupuncturist served to teach me that my preconceptions about healthcare modalities were not valid.

Particularly for treating chronic (rather than acute) health issues, my preference is for holistic treatments because they are less invasive and more natural to the body. However, it should be noted that the use of nutritional supplements, herbs, homeopathy, acupuncture, and other holistic treatments follows the same paradigm as the use of drugs and surgery. With both conventional and holistic medicine, we are using something outside ourselves to facilitate healing. Conventional medical treatments are not harmful when used appropriately.

During a brief stint as a representative for a nutritional products company, I often heard the management describe the pharmaceutical industry in disparaging terms, while they viewed themselves as health saviors motivated solely by a desire to help others. The nutritional products people failed to recognize that both they and the pharmaceutical companies were operating from the same fundamental belief: that we must take certain substances to maintain or regain our health. Ultimately I chose to disassociate myself from the nutritional company not because of the products, which were of high quality, but due to its marketing approach.

I was drawn to the business initially because nearly everyone I met there seemed motivated by a desire to help people improve their health and well-being. Then the company started promoting their anti-aging supplements by telling potential customers that no matter how good they might look and feel at the moment, if they were over the age of 30, their bodies were "crumbling from the inside out." I knew that the fear-based marketing messages would do more harm than the products did good, and it would have violated my integrity to continue to promote them. Unfortunately, fear-based marketing is widely used in numerous industries because it often is very successful.

There is nothing wrong with using conventional or holistic healthcare services and products; they are useful tools. The crucial point is to realize they are *only* tools – something to help us believe we can heal ourselves, which we have the ability to do on our own.

The Effectiveness of Treatments

Often the easiest way to accomplish something is to use a readily available product or process. Virtually any method can work, within the confines of the belief system of that method. For instance, I believe that aspirin usually relieves a tension headache; it is a method that has worked for me for most of my life. While I know aspirin is not really necessary to relieve headache pain, given my beliefs, often the most efficient course of action when I have a headache is to take an aspirin. The same principle applies to anti-aging products and methods. Usually the most efficient means of achieving a desired result is to follow the path of least resistance.

Individuals' reactions to all types of treatments are tremendously influenced by their expectations. When we are ready to make a change, we draw into our experience something that enables us to believe we can make that change. For instance, a person who is ready to be relieved of an allergy will find a treatment (which could be anything from acupuncture to allergy shots) that seems to eradicate it, or at least successfully treat the symptoms. I use the term "seems to" because the person actually eliminated the allergy herself – and had the ability to do so with or without treatment. The value of taking a physical action is that it can serve as a focal point for directing one's energy.

Conversely, someone who is not ready to be relieved of a health problem will have disappointing (or at best, temporary) results from any treatment. Why, you may wonder, would anyone *not* want to eliminate a health problem such as an allergy? There are many possible reasons. Perhaps the allergy gives the person a reason not to engage in certain activities, or it reinforces his view of himself as a sensitive person. The allergy may be an external representation of the inner sensitivity he feels toward his environment. In many cases, longstanding health and personal problems are incorporated by the ego as part of its identity. If you continue to think of yourself as a person with allergies, it is unlikely that you will eliminate them completely unless you change your self-image.

In both conventional and holistic medicine, there has been an increasing awareness that mental and emotional factors play a role in disease and healing. Regrettably, this realization has led to an artificial separation in which some health problems are considered physical (due to faulty genes, bad luck, or an unhealthy lifestyle) and others are believed to be at least partially mental or emotional in origin. Folks with problems in the latter category (as well as those deemed to have a poor lifestyle) often feel their illness is somehow their fault. In truth, all health problems (including infectious diseases and injuries) start first in the mind. Everything in our experience we create internally and project into the physical world, which includes our bodies. I prefer to eliminate the "fault and blame" question entirely because it is irrelevant and counterproductive. If each of us has created everything in our experience, then all of it is "our fault"! Passing judgment on ourselves and others is not useful.

An obvious question is why someone would choose experiences that are painful, traumatic, or unpleasant. If we have a choice, why don't all of us create a life that is easy and enjoyable? One might as well ask why everyone who goes to college doesn't choose to major in an easy subject! Most of us have life intentions that are best served by having some challenging experiences. An example is Shari, a woman I know who has overcome numerous health problems (including a life-threatening disease) without resorting to radical medical treatments. When Shari was diagnosed with a severe case of Graves' disease (a thyroid disorder), her doctor said it was imperative that she have the malfunctioning gland removed immediately. Against all medical advice, Shari refused surgery and opted to try a variety of holistic treatments (including energy healing and nutritional therapy) instead. Her doctor called her a fool and told her, "Go home to die." Despite the physician's dire prognosis, less than a year later Shari was free of the disease. She now spends much of her time helping others heal themselves physically and emotionally, significantly improving the quality of their lives. Presuming that Shari came into this life with an intention to assist people with healing, it makes sense that she would have chosen to experience a serious health problem herself.

If everything were easy and trouble-free, it is likely that most of us would be bored. Also there is value in contrast – a warm, sunny day seems even better after a week of cold rain. I have never appreciated being alive and well more than right after the times I survived a life-threatening experience. After a serious car accident that I walked away from without injury, I refused offers for a ride home from work. Instead I chose to walk for 20 minutes to the nearest subway station simply because I could. Despite my sore muscles (from tensing up during the accident), I enjoyed every step of that walk.

A Broader View of Health Issues

It is commonly believed that some health problems are purely physical, while others are (at least partially) mentally or emotionally based, perhaps even "psychosomatic." In fact, all health problems are mind-based: outer manifestations of one's inner state. Injuries and illnesses do not happen by chance or just because a person was exposed to disease-causing microbes. A health problem can be viewed as a signal, a message from the inner self. In many cases, the nature of the communication can be determined simply by considering what the affected area of the body represents. Lower back discomfort frequently indicates a lack of support, while pain in the upper back and shoulders may reflect a person's feeling that life is a burden. Foot problems can reveal a fear of moving forward; knee problems may reflect a lack of flexibility.

Some physical associations are humorous. Urinary tract infections, for instance, commonly are a sign that the sufferer is "pissed off" about something. (When I developed a urinary tract infection and a blocked tear duct in the same week, I could only conclude that I was pissed off and holding back tears!) One man noticed that his neck ached whenever he had to deal with a client he thought of as "a pain in the neck." A writer who could not possibly have been pregnant had symptoms of pregnancy that perplexed her until she realized they were a representation of the book she was trying to "birth." A helpful resource for determining the meaning and potential causes of various health conditions is Louise L. Hay's classic little book, *Heal Your Body*[18] The descriptions are not necessarily appropriate for every health condition (each of us has our own internal "language"), but the book is a good starting point.

Communications from the inner self also manifest in our environment, particularly in homes and automobiles. Since water often represents emotions, plumbing problems frequently relate to emotional issues. (A clogged pipe may reflect an emotional block, for example.) When a friend of mine was looking for a home in a new area, he noticed that every house he looked at had mold in the crawl space, as did the house he had just sold (which should not have been prone to mold because it was in an area with low humidity). My friend also suffered from yeast-related problems in his body. After rejecting yet another potential house due to mold problems, he realized the mold and yeast were indications of festering emotional issues he had been holding onto since childhood.

Another example of this type of correspondence is the time I developed pain in a muscle in the back of my right shoulder that was paralleled by a squeaking sound from the right side of my car's front axle. (If you compare the human body to an automobile, the right shoulder corresponds to the right front wheel area.) I noticed the squeak was loudest when the shoulder was most painful. When the pain was mild, the squeak was hardly noticeable. Eventually I took the car to the dealer to have it repaired. A mechanic replaced and oiled the bearings, but the squeak did not improve – nor did my shoulder.

According to Louise Hay in *Heal Your Body*, "Shoulders represent our ability to carry our experiences in life joyously. We make life a burden by our attitude."[19] The words accurately described my outlook: I had been thinking of my responsibilities and daily tasks as a burden, feeling little joy in life. I set an intention to adjust my attitude, and my shoulder felt a bit better. Soon I took the car back to the dealer, where a top-notch mechanic was assigned to the job. It took him several hours to identify the problem and fix it. Rather than being annoyed that the repair was taking longer than expected, I felt sorry for the mechanic. Unbeknownst to him, he was dealing with more than a simple squeak! This time when I picked up the car, the annoying sound was gone for good. Within a few days, the pain in my shoulder went away as well. When I stopped looking at life as a burden, my attitude change was reflected in both the car and my shoulder.

We typically view illnesses and physical discomfort as negative, but this is not necessarily the case. For most of my life, I have perceived muscle soreness from exercise or bodywork to be a positive sign. It means I am becoming stronger or more flexible, or that constricted areas are returning to their natural state. The soreness may be uncomfortable, but in a way it also feels good. Illnesses, however, I perceived as negative – they were caused by foreign invaders that mercilessly attacked my body. If microbes overcame my defenses and made me sick, I thought the best course of action was to try to fight them off.

Viruses, bacteria, and other microbes are present in our body at all times, but we typically are not aware of them unless they get out of balance and cause noticeable effects that we perceive as illness. These organisms serve a useful purpose, which is why our bodies allow them to be present. Symptoms such as mucous discharge, fever, sweating, and diarrhea are part of the body's cleansing process – the physiological version of a major housecleaning. To impede these processes with medication is counterproductive to the maintenance of health and balance.

Shortly after having this insight, I became sick with flu-like symptoms, which provided me the opportunity to observe how my new perspective affected my experience of illness. While I was not happy about the sore throat, congestion, fever, and muscle aches, I chose to accept these symptoms as part of a necessary and beneficial process. Overall, the illness turned out to be considerably milder than other times I have had the flu. While I do not know for sure that the severity of the illness was affected by the change in my attitude, I suspect it was. To quote an adage, "Whatever we resist persists."

Menopause

Menopause signifies two things: a woman cannot get pregnant anymore and she no longer has menstrual cycles. That is *all* it has to mean. The mood swings, hot flashes, and numerous other symptoms believed to be a natural part of menopause are not inevitable. Even after the ovaries stop producing hormones, the adrenal glands continue to secrete some estrogen, progesterone, and testosterone. These glands are quite capable of producing ample amounts of sex hormones to prevent hormone withdrawal symptoms. (This idea is not just a theory. A friend's mother, who was in her seventies and had never had hormone replacement therapy, was told by a doctor that she had the estrogen level of an average 35-year-old female.)

105

Menopause need not be anything more than a blip on the screen of life. Our society pathologizes it partly due to our negative beliefs about aging and partly because it is a lucrative marketing opportunity. When baby boomers started reaching menopause, this natural event (which already was being treated as a disease) began drawing a great deal of attention. Menopause is not a disease or condition that requires treatment; it is simply a natural stage.

So-called "perimenopause" or "premenopause" is basically a marketing invention. Savvy businesspeople realized that the years between childbearing and menopause were underexploited commercially, so they invented a condition to create a perceived need for products and services during that time. Hormone levels fluctuate throughout life; it does not need to be considered a problem. As a young adult I was amenorrheic (a fancy way of saying "period-free") for over six years. During that time I was told I had the sex hormone levels of a postmenopausal woman, yet I did not suffer from any of the physical and emotional symptoms commonly believed to result from low hormone levels.

If you consider the fundamentals of menopause (the cessation of menstrual cycles and fertility), it is doubtful that most women would have a problem with them. Some younger women take birth control pills almost continuously so they will not become pregnant and rarely have menstrual periods. Menopause gives us these things naturally! It should be a cause for celebration, not distress.

However, the fact that unpleasant menopausal effects are due to beliefs does not mean they are not genuine. All physical conditions are due to beliefs, and when a person is suffering, it is unfair to dismiss her concerns as invalid. Acknowledging that everything we experience is valid helps us have compassion for those in distress – and all of us fall into that category at times.

Reaching menopause actually may be beneficial to a woman's health in some ways. Significant resources (minerals, vitamins, and protein) are expended in preparing the body for potential pregnancy every month. When menstrual cycles stop, these resources can be used for other purposes, such as regenerating the body's cells and tissues.

Energy Healing

Energy healing can be broadly defined as "restoring to a state of balance by means that affect the body's nonphysical energy centers and mind-body energy field" rather than just the physical body. This description covers a wide variety of approaches and practices. Many people have the ability to help others heal, not by fixing what is wrong, but by assisting the person in healing themselves by returning to their natural, healthy state. This ability is innate and does not need to be taught, but in our culture it is widely believed that we must take courses and acquire certifications to use it in a structured way.

Two well known energy-healing modalities are Reiki and Therapeutic Touch, which have been widely used for decades. Both practices involve a practitioner placing his hands on or near the recipient's body. I have had Reiki treatments and felt tangible effects. In my first treatment, the energy emanating from the practitioner's hands was so intense that it felt like a warm iron was next to my skin.

There are many theories about how the various energy therapies work. The developers of some of the most dramatically effective techniques are honest enough to say "I don't know" when asked to explain the mechanism by which they achieve such profound results. My own theory (which I do not claim is accurate) is that in energy therapies such as laying on hands, the practitioner generates a certain vibration and directs it to the recipient. If the recipient allows it, his body entrains to that vibration, resonance occurs, and his system returns to its natural state. To use a musical analogy, it is as if the recipient is singing off key and can't find the right pitch. The practitioner is singing on key and sings the note strongly until

107

the recipient is able to match the note and maintain it on his own. In cases where the practitioner temporarily takes on some of the symptoms of the recipient (which is *not* necessary to facilitate healing) it is as if the practitioner has wavered from the note and gone off key along with the recipient.

Not only is energy healing just as "real" as conventional medical methods, it works on a more fundamental level. It is not uncommon for energy healers to facilitate the healing of a condition that medical professionals have given up on. If I had a serious health issue that could not be handled with acute care services, I would consult an energy therapy practitioner prior to seeking help from a conventional medical practitioner. Too often people consult an energy healer as a last resort, after their bodies have been damaged by invasive medical treatments.

Reality Shifting

Several relatively new energy-healing modalities are yielding results that are nothing short of miraculous. Some of these methods are outside the bounds of my definition of energy healing because they go beyond affecting the mind-body energy field.

Richard Bartlett, DC, ND, founder of Matrix Energetics® (matrixenergetics.com), discovered that by lightly touching his clients while applying focused intent, he could restore them to a physically, mentally, emotionally, and spiritually balanced state, instantly transforming conditions that had troubled them for years.[20] Dr. Bartlett now teaches Matrix Energetics (which he describes as a "consciousness technology" based on quantum physics rather than a technique), and it is being used by many practitioners to facilitate healings so profound that they can best be described as "transformation."

Another groundbreaking modality is Reconnective Healing (the reconnection.com), discovered by Eric Pearl, DC, which accesses frequencies that return the body and mind to a state of balance.[21] These methods and others are being used to achieve remarkable changes.

Self-Help Methods

In addition to the plethora of energy healing services offered by trained practitioners, there are energy therapies that do not require the services of a professional. These methods are especially useful for addressing minor issues. With simple instructions, most people can perform the techniques themselves.

A popular and easy-to-use energy therapy is *acupressure*, the practice of applying pressure to specific points on the surface of the body to increase energy, alleviate pain, and restore the body to optimal functioning. Acupressure is sometimes called *reflexology*, although the latter term is more often used to refer specifically to acupressure performed on the feet and hands. A good resource for learning acupressure is the book *Body Reflexology: Healing at Your Fingertips* by Mildred Carter and Tammy Weber.[22]

A Healthy Environment

All information regarding what is good and bad for our health is based upon beliefs, and in this book I have made a sincere effort to avoid presenting beliefs as truths. However, many beliefs regarding health are so strongly held in collective consciousness that it is difficult not to align with them, at least to some degree. It also should be noted that "collective consciousness" is not something outside of ourselves that we are passively subject to. Each of us participates in and contributes to collective consciousness, which is why it is called "collective." When even one individual alters her beliefs, the change affects collective consciousness.

I sometimes refer to our strongly held mass beliefs as "the default." It certainly is possible for an individual to move beyond the default, and many have done so. In *The Holographic Universe*, Michael Talbot presents numerous examples of documented cases of people who have done things that seem to defy what are considered fundamental laws of nature. Yet most of us would find it hard to live for years without food or water, as did German mystic Therese Neumann.[23] Nor could we handle poisonous snakes and drink strychnine (rat poison) and remain unharmed, which is a common practice for some members of Pentecostal Christian churches in the southeastern United States. We can, however, choose to be unaffected by whatever the media is focusing on as the latest scare.

A poignant example of how health fears can adversely affect a person's life is a woman I met who confided in me her terror of asbestos. For a few hours she had been exposed to a low level of asbestos in an office where old ceiling tiles were being replaced. Although her exposure was so minimal that asbestos experts assured her there was no risk to her health, she was plagued by fears she knew were irrational. This healthy, vibrant woman was worrying herself sick over something harmless to her! She is not alone; I have noticed many people following this path. They align with a well-publicized belief about the dangers of something and focus on it to the point that their fear – not the actual substance or disease, but their fear of it – adversely affects their daily life.

How do these situations start? Typically they begin when something is deemed a serious risk to human health. The news media picks up the story, and it peppers our conversations. Soon an industry grows up around the fear: products and services are developed and marketed; and lawyers, health professionals, and insurance companies become involved. Examples of such "fear industries" are cancer detection and treatment, AIDS testing and treatment, asbestos removal, and radon mitigation. What many folks fail to realize is that we do not have to follow the dictates of authorities and the media as if we were sheep! We simply can choose not to pay attention to whatever is being promoted as the latest health hazard.

While it is worthwhile to minimize exposure to toxic chemicals in your daily environment, try not to be too upset about occasional exposures. The stress from worrying about them may do more damage to a healthy person than the toxin itself. As with anything else, notice and heed your body's communications. Move away from things that bother you, which can include not just toxic substances but people and situations you find stressful. As a general rule, however, consider yourself invulnerable to these influences – and you will be.

Tobacco

Beliefs about the harmful effects of certain substances are deeply ingrained in most individuals and collective consciousness, to the point that the simplest option is to limit or avoid using them. Regarding tobacco, Americans have been inundated since the 1960s with data indicating that smoking cigarettes leads to several life-threatening diseases. It would be difficult for someone in the United States to be unaffected by that belief and smoke heavily for years with no adverse effects. (In other countries, less emphasis is placed on the dangers of smoking.) If you can accomplish this feat (with tobacco or anything else), then more power to you! When a friend was considering quitting smoking, I encouraged her by appealing to her vanity. "Forget about lung cancer and emphysema," I said (only half-facetiously); "smoking can cause wrinkles and stain your teeth." In fact, smokers generally do look older than their nonsmoking contemporaries.

Although I have never smoked anything in my life, I acknowledge that other people have the right to make their own choices. If you live with someone who smokes and are bothered by it, arrange to have the person's smoking restricted to limited areas. Beyond that measure, I suggest that when nonsmokers find themselves near a person who is smoking, they ignore it as much as possible. Remember that we attract what we focus on.

Pharmaceutical and Over-the-Counter Drugs

Pharmaceutical drugs are best reserved for short-term use (in cases of acute infection, for example). For chronic health issues, investigate other methods of healing that do more than treat symptoms. If you have been given a prescription, particularly for a drug you expect to take long term, it is worthwhile to learn all you can about it. Read the literature that comes with your prescription and do further research to obtain information from sources other than the manufacturer.

Avoid taking antibiotics unless you have a bacterial infection or are undergoing surgery that may predispose you to infection. This suggestion may seem obvious, yet doctors frequently prescribe antibiotics to treat viral illnesses. Antibiotics destroy not only the bacteria that cause infections, but also the beneficial bacteria in the intestines that are needed for proper digestion. After completing a course of antibiotics, it is a good idea to replace these essential bacteria (often called *probiotics*) by eating yogurt or taking a broad-spectrum probiotic supplement. For at least two weeks after finishing the antibiotics, eat two or three servings per day of plain, unsweetened yogurt, which contains probiotics. Soy-based yogurts are an option for vegans. People who dislike yogurt can opt for probiotic supplements.

Most over-the-counter drugs only treat symptoms and can actually impede healing. For example, reducing a fever can slow your recovery because fever helps the body combat pathogens. Cold remedies that stop a runny nose can hinder the body's cleansing process and cause side effects such as drowsiness or nervousness. Personally, I avoid over-the-counter drugs except for infrequent use of pain relievers.

Chapter 7

Fitness Without a Regimen

~~~

We don't stop playing because we grow old; we grow old because we stop playing.

—George Bernard Shaw (Irish playwright, 1856–1950)

Don't Act Your Age

Physical activity is one of the most important things you can do to maintain or regain youthful functioning. It is not necessary to join a health club, hire a personal trainer, or buy exercise equipment. Just move your body, and do it frequently. To reacquaint yourself with natural movement, observe how children move when they are playing: they sit on the floor or ground, run, jump, and flip over, in an almost endless variety of actions and positions. Compare the movements of children and teenagers to those of adults. You will observe that most adults move more slowly and stiffly, with a limited range of motion. When adults sit on the floor, many find it awkward and uncomfortable. Contrary to common belief, they lost their flexibility not because of advancing age, but due to lack of use.

If you want to look and feel like a young person, move like a young person. Replace some of the chairs in your home with large cushions and sit on the floor regularly. Stay active throughout the day, not just during scheduled exercise periods. If you have a desk job, stand up frequently and walk. Visit coworkers personally rather than using the phone or email. If you are restricted from leaving your desk, get up from your chair and move around. People with jobs that require standing for long periods should look for opportunities to sit, even on a countertop.

Develop an Exercise Habit

For those accustomed to a sedentary lifestyle, the habit of moving the body frequently may not come naturally at first. Exercise is an area where a regular routine serves most of us well. Even if you don't feel particularly energetic, once you take the first few steps it is likely you will get into the mood of exercising. Here are some suggestions for making exercise a regular part of your life:

- Establish a simple routine that includes endurance (cardiovascular) exercise, stretching, and strengthening. It is best to begin with activities that do not require expensive equipment or special clothing. With a minimal financial investment, you will feel free to move on to something else if the first activity you try doesn't suit you.

- Schedule a regular time for exercise. As a general rule, the earlier in the day you exercise, the better. Many people find it easier to follow a morning or midday routine than one in the late afternoon or evening. As the day progress, the chances increase that something will interfere with your schedule.

- Use whatever means are necessary to motivate yourself: a workout partner, exercise class, or fitness book or video. Most importantly, choose activities you enjoy. After getting past the initial discomfort of exercising when you are unaccustomed to it, if you find that you genuinely don't care for a particular activity, switch to another one – but don't quit exercising. In addition, do not force yourself to exercise to the point that it becomes unpleasant or painful. Pushing too hard (especially at first) is likely to make you dread your next exercise session. It also can lead to injuries.

- Follow your new routine for three weeks, doing your best not to skip a scheduled session. It typically takes about 21 days to form (or break) a habit. By the end of the third week, you will be feeling – and perhaps seeing – the benefits of your fitness routine and will want to continue it.

Types of Exercise

Some of the best exercises require the least paraphernalia. Brisk walking and jogging require only a pair of athletic shoes and supportive undergarments. For strengthening, you do not necessarily need to use weights or weight machines. The classic military-style pushup is an excellent strengthening exercise that requires no equipment. Hatha yoga (the branch of yoga that involves the practice of physical postures) is a comprehensive exercise system that stretches and strengthens muscles and connective tissue, improves balance and posture, and tones internal organs. Despite the heavy marketing of yoga-related products, the practice requires nothing more than nonrestrictive clothing and a carpet or mat.

In addition to doing stretching exercises and maintaining general flexibility, one of the best ways to prevent injuries is to avoid performing the same strenuous or high-impact activities on consecutive days. Skipping a day allows the body time to repair any minor damage to muscles and connective tissue.

It is a common belief that people are more prone to injury as they grow older, but this is not necessarily the case. In my teens and twenties, I rarely did stretching and usually performed the same high-impact activities on consecutive days, which led to frequent minor injuries. Eventually I discovered I could maintain the same level of fitness by skipping days between workouts. I revised my fitness program to include stretching exercises and rest days, and also started performing different activities on alternate days. Consequently, I am considerably less injury-prone now than when I was younger.

When your fitness habit is well established, periodically varying your routine can help keep it interesting. While it is beneficial and efficient to have habits that serve our purposes, there is a delicate balance between regularly following routines and being overly rigid. Exercising when you wake up in the morning is a great way to start the day, but occasionally you may want to give yourself a treat by starting the day leisurely with a cup of tea.

Use Your "Other" Hand

Most of us tend to use our dominant hand (for 85 to 90 percent of the population, it is the right hand) for tasks requiring fine coordination. Develop the habit of sometimes using your nondominant hand for opening doors, eating, drinking, using a computer touch pad or mouse, throwing a ball, and other activities for which you normally would use your dominant hand.

The right hand is connected to the brain's left hemisphere, which prefers structured information, letters and symbols; orderliness, and predictability, and is good at learning facts and details. The right hemisphere prefers pictures to symbols, takes a holistic view, and likes spontaneity and surprises. Ideally there should be a balance in our use of the two hemispheres, but modern culture and education tend to favor left brain–dominant activities. By using our nondominant hand, we can help activate the right hemisphere and balance our use of the various brain functions. (Note that in some left-handed people, the functions of the brain hemispheres are reversed from what is described above. It varies among individuals.)

The Tibetan Rites of Rejuvenation

Practices such as hatha yoga and qi gong (an ancient Chinese discipline that stimulates the flow of life force energy by using controlled breathing and movements) affect subtle energies to benefit the mind and body. People who perform these practices regularly seem to age more slowly than their contemporaries. Although the techniques can be learned from books and videos, working with an instructor for initial training can be valuable.

A practice I have found especially beneficial is the Tibetan Rites of Rejuvenation, a yoga-like routine brought to the West in the early 1900s by a British army colonel who spent several years in a Himalayan monastery. The practice became well known in the United States from a book called *Ancient Secret of the Fountain of Youth* by Peter Kelder.[24] The rites (often called the Five Tibetans, despite the existence of an optional sixth rite) are practiced around the world. They are believed to prevent aging by activating the body's nonphysical energy centers. The energy centers or chakras (*chakra* is the Sanskrit word for *wheel* or *disk*) are associated with the endocrine glands. Impaired endocrine function is a significant factor in age-related degeneration; keeping these glands working well helps maintain youthfulness.

There are numerous dramatic reports of rejuvenation and health improvements that have resulted from practicing the Five Tibetans. Kelder's book includes many impressive testimonials from people who report that after consistently practicing the rites for months or years, they look and feel as much as 20 years younger than they did before. These accounts may be valid, but since I cannot attest to their accuracy, I have not included them here. Personally, I have found that practicing the Five Tibetans has increased my strength, flexibility, and balance. A month after I started the practice, I noticed that my senses of hearing and smell (which already were keen) became even sharper. In addition to

117

improving physical fitness and enhancing glandular functioning, practicing the Five Tibetans has the advantage of being fast (under 15 minutes), convenient (the routine can be performed almost anywhere and requires no equipment other than a carpet or mat), and cost-free (except for the possible purchase of a book).

Instructions for the Tibetan Rites

The rites consist of five different movements (with the addition of an optional sixth rite), each of which is performed 21 times. Start with 3 repetitions of each rite, adding 2 or 3 repetitions per week until you work up to the full 21. (As much as possible, do the same number of repetitions of all the rites.) The entire routine can be completed in less than 15 minutes. It is recommended that you perform the rites daily, missing no more than one day per week. Because the exercises are not high-impact or overly strenuous, performing them daily does not lead to injuries.

The daily routine works well for many people, but for those who are unlikely to follow a daily schedule, it is better to practice the rites every second day than not at all. Another option is to do the full 21 repetitions on alternate days and perform only 7 repetitions on the days in between. Doing the routine sporadically, however, will not be effective. If you habitually miss two or more consecutive days, the benefits will diminish. If you are performing the rites daily, I recommend taking off at least one day a month. For menstruating women, the heaviest day of menstruation is a good day to skip.

In addition to following the instructions provided in this chapter, it is a good idea to read one of the books about the rites, which give complete directions and illustrations. *The Five Tibetans* by Christopher S. Kilham not only demonstrates and explains the rites; it provides instructions (included below) for breathing during and between each rite.[25]

In Peter Kelder's book, the description of Rite 6 includes the practice of celibacy. This rite is presented as an optional addition to the other five rites; the exercise portion of Rite 6 is supposed to help control sexual desire. Christopher Kilham says he does not believe celibacy is necessary for maintaining youthfulness, and I agree. My view is that celibacy – while it is a choice of experience as valid as any other – is not a requirement for either rejuvenation or spiritual growth. I have found the exercise portion of Rite 6 to be helpful in strengthening abdominal muscles and organs, but it has not affected my libido at all, possibly because that isn't my intention in performing the rite.

Following is a concise version of the instructions for the Tibetan Rites of Rejuvenation. As with any physical exercise, use common sense when performing the Five Tibetans. If you experience pain or dizziness, slow down or stop. Those under the care of a health practitioner for a serious condition such as a heart problem should check with that person prior to starting an exercise program, including this one.

Breathing – Prior to performing Rite 1 and after completing each rite, stand erect with hands on hips. Inhale deeply through the nose, hold your breath for one or two seconds as you form your lips into the shape of the letter O, and then exhale completely through the mouth. Repeat (for a total of two complete breaths after each rite).

Rite 1 – Stand erect with arms extended straight out to the sides, palms down. Relax the shoulders and raise the arms to be in line with the shoulders. Spin in place in a clockwise direction, as fast as you can without losing control. To prevent dizziness as you spin, focus your vision on a single point straight ahead. Continue to focus on the point until it leaves your field of vision, and then focus on another point. If you feel dizzy, slow down or stop. Start with just a few spins and work up to 21 revolutions.

Rite 2 – Lie flat on the floor, face up with arms fully extended along sides, palms on floor, and fingers together. Raise the head from the floor, tucking the chin to the chest. As you do this, lift the legs (with the knees straight) into a vertical position. Keeping the knees straight, slowly lower the head and legs to the floor simultaneously. Breathing through the nose, inhale deeply as you lift the legs, hold your breath while legs are vertical, and exhale completely as you lower the legs. Work up to 21 repetitions.

Rite 3 – Kneel on the floor with the body erect, toes flexed, and hands on the back of the thighs just under the buttocks. Tilt the head and neck forward, tucking the chin to the chest. Then tilt the head and neck backward, arching the spine backward, and look up. After arching, return to the original position. Breathing through the nose, inhale deeply as you arch the spine, hold your breath while the back is arched, and exhale completely as you return to an erect position. Work up to 21 repetitions.

Rite 4 – Sit on the floor with legs extended, body erect, feet flexed and a little less than shoulder-width apart, palms flat on the floor next to the hips, and fingers pointed toward feet. Tuck the chin to the chest, and then tilt the head backward as far as it can go comfortably. At the same time, bend the knees and push up to a "tabletop" position with the arms straight. Let the head fall back gently. The trunk of the body will be in a straight line, with thighs horizontal to the floor. Tense every muscle in the body. Relax the muscles as you return to the original sitting position. Breathing through the nose, inhale deeply as you rise, hold your breath as you tense the muscles, and exhale completely as you descend. Work up to 21 repetitions.

Rite 5 – Begin face down on all fours with your body straight, toes flexed, hands on the floor, and weight distributed evenly between the palms of hands and the balls of feet (similar to a pushup position). The hands and feet should remain in the same position throughout this rite. Start with arms perpendicular to the floor and spine arched downward, with the body in a sagging position. Slowly lift the buttocks toward the sky with the back flat, lowering the head so the body makes an inverted V. Tuck the chin to the chest. Pause, and then lower the buttocks while pressing palms into the floor until legs are parallel to the ground, moving the chest out and shoulders back. Breathing through the nose, inhale deeply as you raise the body, hold your breath while in the V position, and exhale completely as you come down. Work up to 21 repetitions.

Rite 6 – Stand erect and inhale through the nose. Exhale through the mouth as you bend from the waist, placing hands on knees. Expel as much air from the lungs as you can. Without taking a new breath, return to an erect position. Place hands on hips with fingers to the front, and suck in the abdomen as much as possible. When you must take a breath, inhale through the nose and exhale through the mouth as you drop your arms to your sides to relax. Take several normal breaths through the nose and mouth before beginning again. Work up to 3 repetitions.

Relaxation – After completing the rites, spend a few minutes in a relaxation pose. Lie flat on the floor, face up, with palms facing upward and arms and legs extended but relaxed. Close your eyes and completely relax all your muscles. Breathe deeply and easily through the nose, clearing your mind of thoughts. The relaxation period enables your body and mind to release tension and allows the chakras to come into balance.

Energy Centers (Chakras)

The nonphysical energy centers associated with the body are commonly referred to as *chakras*. There are several major chakras associated with the spinal column, center of the head, and area above the head. Numerous minor chakras exist throughout the body, but this book covers only the major chakras.

The most accurate information I have found about chakras is from an unusual source: an "energy personality essence no longer physically focused" (in common terms, a spirit) named Elias who speaks through a woman named Mary Ennis.[26] In an action similar to what generally is called channeling, Mary Ennis goes into a trance and allows Elias to project through her. His intention is to deliver information with the least possible amount of distortion. Of the vast quantity and variety of metaphysical teachings I have studied, I have found Elias's information to be the most accurate and reliable. Because so much distorted information has been offered about the chakras, Elias prefers to call them energy centers. In this book I use the terms interchangeably.

The information presented here about the chakras is taken directly from the Elias session transcripts. (To access the transcripts, see the websites eliasweb.at and eliasforum.org.) Those with some knowledge of the chakras will notice I include four you may not be familiar with; the colors are pink, white, magenta, and black. The pink chakra is located in the upper chest, between the heart and throat. Elias says this is a new energy center we have developed to aid in movement within other energy centers and to promote healing and psychic activity. The white, magenta, and black chakras are involved in connecting to other areas of consciousness and bringing communications from these areas into physical focus.

Red – Located in the base of the spine. Radiates down. Governs the feet, legs, large intestine, nervous system, spine, teeth, bones, and male and female organs. Associated with grounding, sleep, and meditation. Supports the immune system in conjunction with the green and yellow energy centers. The essence of physical manifestation, this energy center holds great power. Vibrates to the tone *lo* (pronounced "low").

Orange – Located in the genitals. Radiates out. Governs the reproductive organs, kidneys, bladder, adrenal glands, skin, and bodily fluids except blood. Associated with sexual orientation and desire, life giving, and parenting. Vibrates to the tone *mu* (pronounced "moo").

Yellow – Located in the stomach. Radiates out and up. Governs the stomach, gallbladder, liver, small intestine, and pancreas. Associated with breathing (diaphragmatic), singing, all emotions, and detachment. Supports the immune system in conjunction with the red and green energy centers. Vibrates to the tone *wah* (pronounced "waw").

Green – Located in the heart. Radiates up. Governs the blood, circulatory system, heart, hands, arms, lungs, and respiratory system. Associated with the sense of touch, healing, emotion of love transcendent love, bravery, and assertiveness. Supports the immune system in conjunction with the red and yellow energy centers. Vibrates to the tone *ti* (pronounced "tea").

Pink – Located in the upper chest between the heart and throat, is connected with and works in conjunction with the green energy center. Radiates up in conjunction with the green energy center. Associated with healing, connection, calming, and nurturing; helpful in aiding movement within other energy centers. Allows physical incorporation of subjective actualizations and increases in psychic activity. Vibrates to the tone *si* (pronounced "sea").

Blue – Located in the throat. Radiates up. Governs the vocal chords, ears, shoulders, and nervous system. Associated with hearing, communication, loyalty, energy level, outlook, and self-image. Vibrates to the tone *rai* (pronounced "ray").

Indigo – Located in the center of the head, paralleling the space between the eyes. (Traditionally known as "the third eye.") Radiates up. Governs the eyes, nose, ears, head, and brain. Associated with bodily expressions, energy exchange, thought, intuition, and creativity. Vibrates to the tone *whou* (pronounced "hwoo," with emphasis on the "h").

Purple – Located on the top of the head, actually centered outside the physical body. Radiates up and down. Associated with spirituality, psychic energy, and physically focused consciousness. Directs all other energy centers. Vibrates to the tone *mai* (pronounced "may").

White – Located above the head, slightly to the left-hand side. Vibrates to the tone *som* (pronounced "sum"). Connects with broader areas of consciousness.

Magenta – Located above the head, directly above the purple energy center. Vibrates to the tone *ra* (pronounced "rah"). Connects with broader areas of consciousness.

Black – Located above the head, slightly to the right-hand side. Vibrates to the tone *nah* (pronounced "naw"). Connects with broader areas of consciousness.

Balancing and Aligning the Chakras

When the chakras are balanced and aligned, our body and mind functions optimally. Chakras are affected by numerous nonphysical factors including our beliefs and personal issues. (Fears about security, for instance, can manifest as problems with the red chakra. Difficulties with communication can lead to problems with the blue chakra.) The yellow chakra (associated with emotions) is the one most commonly out of alignment. The most effective way to balance a misaligned chakra long-term is to address the underlying issues.

Practices such as visualization and toning (using the human voice to release tensions and restore the body to a balanced, healthy state) also can be helpful for chakra realignment and balancing. Each chakra resonates with a particular musical note or pitch, which varies slightly among individuals. As a general rule, the note (pitch) for the red chakra is the lowest. As you move up the body, the notes become progressively higher.

Each chakra can be visualized as a sphere rotating in a clockwise direction, with the spine as the axis. (To clarify what *clockwise* means in this context, if a person standing above you could look down and see your chakras, he would observe the spheres rotating in a clockwise direction.)

The chakras rotate at different speeds. As you move up the body, the rate of spin increases (red is the slowest and purple the fastest). To balance the chakras, however, it is best to visualize them all spinning at the same rate. To increase your energy level if you have been feeling lethargic, visualize the chakras spinning rapidly. To calm yourself and reduce anxiety, visualize them spinning more slowly.

Study the descriptions of the various chakras and the organs and characteristics they govern. You can use this information to develop visualization techniques tailored to your individual needs. Following is an energy center visualization adapted from information given in the Elias sessions[27]

1) Visualize each energy center as a small ball, and imagine a white string or mist that moves through the energy center and connects it to the one above it.

2) Start with the red energy center. While toning (aloud or mentally) the sound *lo* (low), visualize a red sphere spinning clockwise at the base of your spine.

3) As you move from one energy center to the next, visualize the lower energy centers continuing to rotate, all at the same speed, and visualize the white mist moving upward.

4) Move up the body to the orange energy center. While toning *mu* (moo), visualize an orange sphere spinning clockwise on your spine at the level of the lower abdomen.

5) Move up to the yellow energy center. While toning *wah* (waw), visualize a yellow sphere spinning clockwise on your spine at the level of the stomach.

6) Move up to the green energy center. While toning *ti* (tea), visualize a green sphere spinning clockwise on your spine at the level of the heart.

7) Move up to the pink energy center. While toning *si* (sea), visualize a pink sphere spinning clockwise on your spine at the level of the breastbone.

8) Move up to the blue energy center. While toning *rai* (ray), visualize a blue sphere spinning clockwise on your spine at the level of the throat.

9) Move up to the indigo energy center. While toning *whou* (hwoo), visualize an indigo sphere spinning clockwise in the center of your head at eye level.

10) Move up to the purple energy center. While toning *mai* (may), visualize a purple sphere spinning clockwise just above the crown of your head.

11) Move up to the white energy center. While toning *som* (sum), visualize a white sphere spinning clockwise above your head, slightly to your left.

12) Move to the magenta energy center, which is to the right of the white energy center and directly above the purple one. While toning *ra* (rah), visualize a magenta sphere spinning clockwise above the purple energy center.

13) Move to the black energy center, which is to the right of the magenta energy center, at about the same level as the white one. While toning *nah* (naw), visualize a black sphere spinning clockwise above your head, slightly to your right.

14) As you complete your visualization of the energy centers and the rising white mist, allow the mist to penetrate throughout your body. Visualize it gently falling over your body as if you were standing in a light, misty rain.

Chakra Visualization with the Tibetan Rites

After learning about the chakras, I combined the energy center balancing visualization with the practice of the Five Tibetans. Rather than counting the repetitions, I kept track of them by sequentially visualizing each chakra and mentally toning the related sound. Using this method, I perform 22 rather than 21 repetitions of each rite. Although the basic instructions call for only 21 repetitions, there is no harm in performing an extra one. If you use this method, remember to visualize each chakra spinning in a clockwise direction, with your spine as the axis. (In this context, *clockwise* means that if a person standing above you could look down and see your chakras, she would observe the spheres rotating in a clockwise direction.) As you concentrate on each successive chakra, imagine all the other chakras continuing to spin at the same rate.

Repetition 1 – Mentally tone *lo* (low) while visualizing a red sphere spinning at the base of your spine.

Repetition 2 – Mentally tone *mu* (moo) while visualizing an orange sphere spinning in your lower abdomen.

Repetition 3 – Mentally tone *wah* (waw) while visualizing a yellow sphere spinning in your stomach area.

Repetition 4 – Mentally tone *ti* (tea) while visualizing a green sphere spinning in your heart area.

Repetition 5 – Mentally tone *si* (sea) while visualizing a pink sphere spinning in your upper chest.

Repetition 6 – Mentally tone *rai* (ray) while imagining a blue sphere spinning in your throat area.

Repetition 7 – Mentally tone *whou* (hwoo) while imagining an indigo sphere spinning in the center of your head, just above eye level.

Repetition 8 – Mentally tone *mai* (may) while imagining a purple sphere spinning just above the crown of your head.

Repetition 9 – Mentally tone *som* (sum) while imagining a white sphere spinning above your head, on your left-hand side.

Repetition 10 – Mentally tone *ra* (rah) while imagining a magenta sphere spinning above your head, directly above the purple chakra.

Repetition 11 – Mentally tone *nah* (naw) while imagining a black sphere spinning above your head, on your right-hand side.

Repetitions 12 through 22 – Follow the above sequence in reverse, starting with the black chakra (described in Repetition 11) and ending with the red chakra (described in Repetition 1).

Chapter 8

Nutrition Without a Diet Plan

~~~

What is food to one, is to others bitter poison.

—Lucretius (Roman poet and philosopher, 99 BC–55 BC)

What (and When) to Eat

Dietary recommendations typically are based on the assumption that most people's nutritional requirements are pretty much the same, which clearly is not the case. Everyone with a digestive system is an alchemist: we transmute the foods we eat into completely different substances, which can vary tremendously from person to person.

I have done a great deal of research on nutrition and diet, and ultimately came to the conclusion that nobody has "the answer" to the question of optimum diet – simply because there isn't one. At one point I read three books on a well-established health and nutrition system; each book was authored by a recognized expert in the field. I was amused to find significant contradictions in the information given by the three experts, and this was within the same system! Various systems can be helpful as a starting point, but ultimately it is the individual who is the true expert. For this reason, most of the suggestions I offer about nutrition are general in nature. My intention is not to create yet another belief system about diet.

The optimum diet for each person is matching food choices to the individual's vibrational quality. The best way to do this is to pay attention to your preferences and notice how particular foods affect you. We change constantly, so it is important to be open to varying your diet and trying new foods. Those that were your favorites in the past might not be appropriate for you now. To make optimal food choices, pay attention to what (and when) you truly feel like eating. Unfortunately, sometimes it is hard to tell the difference between an intuitive feeling that you need a particular food and a craving based on an unhealthy dependency. (It is possible to become dependent on a substance like refined sugar, which affects some people like a drug.)

A good method for making dietary choices is to ask yourself not only what you feel like eating, but also how you *expect to feel* after you have eaten a food. If you do not think you will feel good after eating it, then don't eat it! Consume only foods you feel positive about putting into your body. All that being said, it is of the utmost importance to enjoy what you eat, so don't choke down something objectionable just because it is supposed to be good for you. Personally, I like desserts (especially chocolate), but prefer a moderate amount of a high-quality treat rather than a large amount of something I consider junk food. Enjoying a few premium cookies or a slice of homemade cherry pie is different from furtively bolting down a bag of greasy potato chips or synthetic-tasting candy.

Regarding diet and aging, the theory with the most supporting evidence is that eating less food leads to decreased degeneration and greater longevity. This doesn't mean you should starve yourself, but erring on the side of smaller portions is a good idea. Eat when you are hungry and only when you are hungry, regardless of what time it is. Following set mealtimes is simply a convention. It takes about 20 minutes for the body to produce signals of fullness, so stop eating before you feel full. Eat several small meals throughout the day rather than one or two large ones. When you consume a large quantity of food at one sitting, more is stored as fat than if you had eaten the same amount at different times throughout the day.

Stuffing yourself with food is not a good practice, but neither is habitually ignoring hunger signals and repeatedly going for long periods without eating. (An occasional one-day fast, however, can be beneficial for people without serious health problems.) Skipping meals in an effort to lose weight is counterproductive. When you have not had nourishment for several hours and are feeling strong hunger pangs, chemical messages alert your brain that you are in danger of starving. The next time you eat, your body tries to conserve as many calories as possible as a hedge against starvation.

The digestive process begins in the mouth. Take small bites, chew slowly, and pay attention to the flavor and texture of what you are eating. Avoid watching television or engaging in intense conversations while you are eating. (Postpone heated debates until well after the meal!) Awareness of the eating process enables you to feel satisfied with a smaller amount of food than if you bolted down your meal half-consciously. It is best to be in a relaxed state before, during, and after eating. Avoid eating when you are feeling very stressed or upset. In stressful situations, the body shunts the blood supply away from the digestive organs, so a meal eaten when you are stressed is not digested properly. If you pay attention, you probably will notice that eating when you are emotionally upset often gives you indigestion.

Special Dietary Concerns

Vegetarianism Versus Nonvegetarianism

The human digestive system appears to have been designed for a primarily plant-based diet; our organs are more like those of an herbivore (animal that feeds primarily on plants) than a carnivore (meat-eater). The digestive tract of carnivorous animals is short (about three times the length of the body) and relatively smooth, which facilitates rapid digestion. Human intestines are approximately 12 times the length of the body and are designed for slower digestion, which is necessary to break down and assimilate nutrients from plant matter. Our dental structure also is best suited to a plant-based diet. Most of our teeth are incisors (for cutting) and molars (for grinding) rather than the sharp canine teeth carnivores use to tear flesh. We do, however, have the capacity to digest and assimilate animal-based foods as well, and people in some cultures thrive on a diet that consists mostly of animal products. Vibrationally, the main difference between foods derived from plants and those from animal sources is their density: animal-derived foods are denser than plants. I expect that as humans continue to evolve, we will choose to consume more plant-based foods because we will become less compatible with the denser animal foods.

All forms of life, including plants, are sentient beings. In my view, it is not inherently wrong to consume animal-derived foods as long as the creatures that have given their lives for our nourishment are treated with respect, compassion, and appreciation. People of more "primitive" cultures hunted animals for food and their hides, but they did so with respect and appreciation for the creatures who gave their lives for the humans' nourishment, warmth, and shelter. Confining chickens to cages, veal calves to tiny pens, and cows to feed lots does not constitute "respect and compassion"! If you choose to consume animal-derived foods, know the source of those foods. Factory-farmed beef, for instance, not only is likely to contain hormones, antibiotics, and other contaminants, it is imbued with the vibrations of fear and suffering the animal endured during its life. Aside from the ethical implications of contributing to cruelty to animals by supporting such industries, do you really want this tainted meat to become part of your own body? Become, literally, a *conscious* consumer.

Genetically Engineered Foods

The concept of balance and harmony as a basic requirement is a belief that is fundamental to humanity. Technological alterations to nature are not inherently beneficial or harmful; it depends upon how well they fit into the larger scheme of things. In some cases, the indications are compelling that the eventual outcome is likely to be detrimental. Genetically engineered foods fall into this category. In foods with genetically modified organisms (GMOs), the genetic material has been modified to enhance specific traits such as growth rate, appearance, flavor, shelf life, or resistance to disease or pests.

An important factor to consider in the GMO controversy is that GMOs result in a loss of diversity within species – and diversity is fundamental to the way nature works. It is virtually impossible to prevent genetically altered plants from pollinating other plants; there have been several cases in which organic crops were found to be contaminated by GMOs from genetically altered plants in nearby fields. Unexpected effects of GMOs have already become evident. (One of the most publicized cases involved the death of monarch butterflies from genetically modified corn.) In addition, it is very likely that genetic modifications alter the vibrational quality – and therefore the nutritional value – of plants in ways scientists do not yet understand.

The issue of GMOs in the food supply concerns me, yet I realize that giving attention to worst-case scenarios is counterproductive because it makes the dire possibilities more likely to occur. Rather than focusing on potential disasters, I find it more constructive to put my energy and money into supporting companies not involved in any way with genetically altered foods.

Organic Foods

Other than growing all your own food (which is impractical for most of us), the best way to ensure you are not consuming foods with GMOs or pesticides is to buy products that are certified organic. At least at this point, your chances of avoiding GMOs are exponentially better if you choose organic foods. (As of this writing, most organic crops have not been contaminated with GMOs, and laws in the United States and many other countries still uphold organic standards.) In addition, you will not be supporting companies that are proponents of genetically engineered foods. Buy meat, eggs, dairy, and other animal products only from producers that treat the creatures with respect. Such companies usually mention these policies on their product packaging.

Organically grown vegetables and fruits also are more nutritious than those grown with pesticides. Plants use flavonoids (potent antioxidants with numerous health benefits) to protect themselves from insects. If pesticides are used, the plants are less likely to produce the highest levels of these nutrients. Comparison tests between organic and conventional fruits and vegetables consistently show flavonoid levels to be significantly higher in organic produce.

Organic and animal-friendly products often cost more than conventional ones, but the effects of supporting these companies extend far beyond your own dinner table. If you are inclined to settle for conventional rather than organic food due to the higher cost of organics, think of the extra money spent as a contribution to several worthy causes. Buying organics supports small, independent farms (the major suppliers of organic products), the well-being of farm workers (who will not be exposed to pesticides, herbicides, and chemical fertilizers), and the humane treatment of animals. Organic production systems preserve and restore natural ecosystems, keeping the soil, water, and air free from toxic chemicals. When you patronize companies that operate with respect for humans, animals, and the environment, you are "voting with your wallet" to support these policies. In my view, this is by far the most effective type of voting.

Nutritional Sources

Plant Foods

Fresh fruits and vegetables contain a wide variety of vitamins, minerals, and other biologically active compounds such as flavonoids and carotenoids (plant pigments ranging from yellow to orange to red), many of which have yet to be isolated in laboratories. Like the flavonoids, carotenoids are potent antioxidants with numerous health benefits. Specific carotenoids such as lutein and zeaxanthin (both are found in high concentrations in kale, spinach, and other dark green leafy vegetables) are especially good for clear vision and eye health. Bilberries also are high in lutein. Lycopene (found in red vegetables and fruits) is beneficial for the vascular system and has anticancer effects, particularly for the prostate.

Anthocyanins (flavonoids in plant pigments ranging from blue to violet to red) have numerous benefits as well. The anthocyanins in blueberries can enhance brain function and help prevent cognitive decline. Açai (pronounced "ah-sigh-ee") berries, which come from a palm tree that grows in Central and South America, have a wide range of anthocyanins and other flavonoid compounds that have been shown to increase endurance, boost the immune system, and have anti-inflammatory effects. Ellagic acid (a phenolic compound found in nuts and fruits, particularly red raspberries) has antimicrobial and anticancer properties and also helps alleviate symptoms of gout. The chlorophyll in green plants acts an anti-inflammatory agent, promotes healthy bowel function, helps prevent infections, and neutralizes some carcinogens. If your daily diet does not include at least six servings of fruits and vegetables, consider using a whole food supplement made from high-nutrient plants.

Other plant foods that are beneficial to include in your regular diet are whole grains, beans, nuts, seeds, and sprouted seeds. Flaxseeds and flaxseed meal are excellent fiber sources that are high in omega-3 oils and easier to digest than bran or psyllium seed. There are many delicious whole grains besides the familiar wheat, rye, and barley. These less-known grains include amaranth, kashi (also called buckwheat, which is not related to wheat), millet, quinoa (pronounced "keen-wa"), and spelt. For commercially prepared breads, an excellent option is a flourless, sprouted whole grain bread (available in the refrigerated section of natural foods stores).

Plant foods are best eaten raw or lightly cooked, as heat can change the vibrational quality of the food and destroy some of the nutrients. With some vegetables (such as broccoli and carrots), light cooking methods such as steaming can increase the bioavailability of nutrients by breaking down some of the cellulose. People unaccustomed to eating raw or lightly cooked foods should increase the proportion of these foods in their diet gradually to allow their digestive system to adjust to the change.

Essential Fatty Acids

Essential fatty acids (EFAs), also known as omega-3, omega-6, and omega-9 oils, are necessary nutrients for the brain, eyes, skin, and hair, as well as for proper hormonal function. Low levels of EFAs can lead to a range of health problems including dry skin, constipation, and depression. If you do not eat flaxseeds, hempseeds, oily fish such as salmon, or other EFA-rich foods frequently, you may want to take EFA supplements in liquid or capsule form. If using fish oil, make sure the product label says it has been purified by molecular distillation, which is the most effective way to remove the impurities and toxins concentrated in fish oil.

Hempseed oil is one of the best plant-based sources of a balanced array of all three types of omega oils. Unlike some fish oils, it also is environmentally friendly. Hempseed oil and hempseeds (a tasty and nutritious snack) have none of the mind-altering effects of marijuana. (In addition, hemp fiber is an ecologically excellent alternative to paper and cotton.) Other excellent plant sources of EFAs are flax and borage oils, which work well in combination. The best formulas include flax lignans (phytochemicals that are strong antioxidants and help balance sex hormone levels.).

Sweeteners

A diet high in refined sugar can contribute to a variety of problems such as blood sugar disorders and mood swings. Refined sugar is listed in many ways on product labels; some of the most common are corn syrup, brown rice syrup, fructose, and maltodextrose.

The artificial sweetener aspartame (brand name NutraSweet®) tends to trigger a craving for sweet foods, which makes it ineffective as a weight loss aid and inappropriate for diabetics. Reactions to this substance vary greatly among individuals. Some people tolerate it without obvious ill effects, but in others it acts like a poison. With my first taste of aspartame, I knew it did not agree with me and made a point of avoiding it. One time I inadvertently ate a cup of aspartame-sweetened yogurt, and about an hour later had an attack of headache, nausea, weakness, and dizziness so severe that I almost fainted. Most people do not react this strongly to the substance, but adverse reactions are not uncommon.

The naturally derived sweeteners stevia and xylitol are excellent alternatives to sugar and artificial sweeteners; both are safe for diabetics. Stevia (which comes from the leaves of the stevia rebaudiana plant) has antimicrobial properties and contains compounds that help regulate blood sugar. Xylitol (found in the fibers of many fruits and vegetables, as well as corn plants and birch trees) has antimicrobial properties and helps strengthen bones and teeth. Both stevia and xylitol are available in powder and liquid forms and also are ingredients in numerous foods, beverages, and dental care products.

Honey is another natural sweetener with health benefits. It has a high glycemic index (causes a rapid rise in blood sugar) and therefore is not appropriate for diabetics, but this effect is moderated when it is combined with other foods. Honey also has antimicrobial properties, eases coughs, and can be applied topically to help heal wounds.

Nutritional Supplements

Nutritional supplements offer many benefits, but conventional vitamin pills are of questionable value. Most such products do not contain the cofactors and synergistic compounds found in whole foods, and in many cases supplements are not properly assimilated by the body. Researchers are continually discovering substances in foods that are beneficial to human health. These compounds work synergistically, so taking only those that have been identified and isolated into supplements does not provide complete nutrition. In addition, there is a vibrational, energetic quality to certain substances that nourishes our bodies, which is why synthetic supplements often don't do much good. They may simulate the chemical structure of selected nutrients, but they lack the vibrational qualities of whole foods.

To test whether the capsules and tablets I was taking were actually being broken down in my stomach, I placed one of each in a small cup of vinegar (which has pH similar to digestive juices) and gently shook the cups to simulate peristalsis. (All the capsules were vegetarian – derived from vegetable cellulose rather than gelatin, which comes from animal connective tissue.) The capsules dissolved at least partially in less than 30 minutes, as did two of the tablets. However, two other tablets (a multivitamin supplement and an herbal blend) remained mostly intact after several hours in the vinegar. Both were fairly expensive brands. This experiment was not ideal because the cup (unlike a stomach) was partially stationary, and the vinegar was at room temperature rather than body temperature. Nevertheless, I was disturbed by the results and quit taking the supplements that did not dissolve. My experiment led me to the disturbing conclusion that many supplements in tablet form are little more than placebos.

Superior alternatives to vitamin pills are whole food supplements made from nutrient-rich plants such as wheat grass, barley grass, alfalfa, spirulina, chlorella, blue-green algae, and deeply pigmented fruits and vegetables. High-quality brands of these products contain complete nutritional complexes the body can assimilate, as well as enzymes needed by the digestive system. There is a tremendous difference in the quality and ingredients of various brands of whole food supplements, so check labels carefully. Avoid products that contain sugar-like sweeteners (such as maltodextrose, barley malt, or brown rice syrup) or large amounts of "filler" ingredients like flax meal, oat bran, rice bran, apple fiber, or lecithin.

Two exceptions to my suggestion about avoiding vitamin supplements are vitamin D and vitamin B_{12}. People who do not have frequent sun exposure on unprotected skin should make sure they eat a diet rich in vitamin D or take a supplement of vitamin D_3 (cholecalciferol), the most easily absorbed form. Folks who do not consume animal products are likely to benefit from vitamin B_{12} supplements.

Minerals

While I do not recommend most vitamin supplements, at times it can be beneficial to take minerals. Unlike water-soluble vitamins, however, minerals accumulate in the body, so it is important not to take too high a dosage. Following are several minerals I have found to be helpful, listed in the forms that are most easily assimilated by the body. Supplementing with minerals is not necessarily appropriate for every individual. I am listing these four because I personally have experienced good results from taking them. Chromium helped stabilize my blood sugar and moods, and magnesium improved my digestion and energy level. After several months of taking sulfur and silica, my hair became thicker.

Chromium picolinate – Chromium is an essential trace mineral that helps stabilize blood sugar. Since chromium is used to metabolize carbohydrates, a high-sugar diet often results in a chromium deficiency. Low chromium levels also are implicated in "atypical" depression (the type of depression that involves low self-esteem, overeating, and sleeping too much rather than anxiety and insomnia). Chromium-rich foods include brewer's yeast, whole grains, and potatoes. The recommended minimum daily intake of chromium is 200 micrograms, but those with low blood sugar, depression, or a tendency for weight gain may want to increase their daily intake to 400 or 600 micrograms.

Magnesium – Magnesium is an essential mineral (the fourth most abundant mineral in the body) that plays a role in more than 300 enzymatic reactions in human metabolism. About 50 percent of the body's magnesium is stored in the bones, and bones cannot metabolize calcium properly without adequate magnesium. It is likely that osteoporosis is due more to lack of magnesium (or an imbalance in calcium and magnesium levels) than to lack of calcium. If you take a calcium supplement, take twice the amount of magnesium (for instance, 600 milligrams of magnesium with 300 milligrams of calcium). In most bone-health supplements that ratio is reversed, so read labels carefully. Magnesium-rich foods include all types of nuts and seeds, most beans, and leafy green vegetables. The recommended minimum daily intake of magnesium is 300 to 400 milligrams, but most people in industrialized countries consume significantly less than this amount. Signs of magnesium deficiency include low energy, fatigue, nervous tension, sleep difficulties, constipation, weak bones, and dental problems.

Methylsulfonylmethane (MSM) – A form of sulfur, MSM can strengthen and rebuild connective tissue, skin, hair, and nails. It also is believed to have a detoxifying effect on many types of cells, keep cell walls flexible and elastic, and promote enzyme production in the body. MSM helps relieves inflammation and joint pain and is commonly taken by people with osteoarthritis, rheumatoid arthritis, and allergies. A typical daily does of MSM is 3 grams.

Vegetal silica – Silica is an essential mineral that is important for healthy skin, hair, nails, connective tissue, bones, and teeth. Silica supplements come in a variety of forms, but vegetal silica, which comes from a plant called shavegrass or horsetail (so named because the plant resembles a horse's tail), may be the most easily assimilated. A typical daily dose of horsetail is 1200 milligrams.

Herbs

The plant kingdom offers an abundance of herbs that are beneficial for various conditions or can be taken as tonics to promote overall wellness. While herbs are not a requirement for maintaining good health or youthfulness, I have used them with good results at various times in my life. There is an energetic synergy between natural substances and the human body, which generally makes herbs more beneficial and less likely to cause harm than drugs used for the same purposes. Many of the medicinal herbs (such as Echinacea and goldenseal) are best used for short periods rather than continuously. Tonic herbs can be taken long-term.

Following are several tonic herbs considered especially good for maintaining youthful well-being. The brief descriptions are only a partial list of each plant's potential benefits. Like most herbs, they are best taken at least half an hour before eating or two hours after a meal. Some are available in herbal teas, which can be used at any time.

Ashwagandha (winter cherry) – In Ayurvedic medicine, ashwagandha is used to promote rejuvenation and longevity. It is known for a broad range of benefits including reduced inflammation, enhanced brain function, improved stress management ability, and greater energy and vitality.

Bhringaraj (eclipta alba) – In Ayurvedic and Chinese medicine, bhringaraj is known for maintaining and enhancing hair color and fullness, improving skin, and rejuvenating teeth, bones, and vision.

Gotu kola – In Ayurvedic and Chinese medicine, gotu kola (which does not contain caffeine) is known for improving circulation, strengthening collagen and connective tissue, enhancing hair strength and fullness, and promoting rejuvenation and longevity.

Gynostemma – Widely used in Asia for promoting rejuvenation and longevity, gynostemma is known for a broad range of health benefits including greater energy and vitality, improved stress management ability, a stronger immune system, enhanced fat metabolism, and better digestion.

He shou wu (fo ti) – In Chinese medicine, he shou wu (which translates to "Mr. Wu's hair stays black") is known for maintaining and enhancing hair color and fullness, improving skin, and rejuvenating teeth, bones, and vision.

Triphala – An Ayurvedic formula, triphala (a blend of the fruits amalaki, bibhilaki, and haritaki) is known for normalizing bowel function and helping detoxify and regenerate numerous body systems. One of triphala's components, amalaki, is a natural source of vitamin C. Since triphala is an intestinal cleanser, start with a low dose (500 milligrams one or two times a day) and gradually increase the dose and/or frequency. If using triphala long term, take at least a one-week break every month.

Wonderful Water

The importance to health of drinking an ample quantity of pure water can hardly be overemphasized. As a general rule, most people should drink two to three liters or quarts of water daily. For a rough estimate of the minimum amount of water to drink each day, estimate 1 liter of water for every 30 kilograms of body weight. (Example: 75 kilograms divided by 30 kilograms equals 2.5, so a person who weighs 75 kilograms should drink at least 2.5 liters of water per day.) To calculate the quantity of water in ounces, divide pounds of body weight by two. (Example: 150 divided by 2 equals 75, so a person who weighs 150 pounds should drink at least 75 ounces of water per day.) These formulas are not exact (the metric formula results in a slightly higher figure), but they provide a general idea. Hot weather, strenuous exercise, and eating salty foods increases your fluid requirements, sometimes markedly. People in high-altitude regions also need to drink more water.

Keep in mind that these quantity suggestions are general in nature and do not necessarily apply to everyone. The water present in foods counts too. If you eat a lot of fruit or other water-heavy foods, you may not need to drink as much water. Like every physical requirement, the need for water varies not only among individuals; it fluctuates in the same person from day to day. Develop a sensitivity to your body's needs by noticing when you are thirsty, hungry, or sleepy. If you have become accustomed to not getting enough fluid and are in a continual state of dehydration, thirst may not be an accurate indicator of how much water you should drink. Unless you are already drinking a lot of water, try increasing your consumption (especially first thing in the morning) by one cup per day and notice if you feel better and have more energy. I have discovered that when I feel fatigued for no apparent reason, it often is due to dehydration.

The body must warm up cold liquids before they can be absorbed, so it is preferable to drink water that is tepid or warm. Cold drinks also can interfere with digestion, especially when taken with meals. Restaurants in the United States typically serve ice water, so make point of requesting water without ice when you are dining out. It can be beneficial to drink hot water occasionally because it has a cleansing effect on the digestive system. To help alleviate constipation, drink a cup of hot water with lemon juice when you wake up in the morning. Do not, however, drink or cook with hot tap water, which may contain dissolved impurities from the pipes and water heater.

It is best to drink water that comes from a natural spring or well or has been distilled or filtered by reverse osmosis. There is an ongoing controversy about the benefits and risks of drinking tap water versus bottled water. In most areas of the United States, municipally supplied tap water contains chlorine, added fluoride, and other impurities, including traces of pharmaceutical drugs. Many plastic water bottles (in addition to being environmentally unfriendly) contain chemicals that may leach into the water and act as hormone disruptors. I am disinclined to enter into the bottled water controversy other than to say that my personal preference is to avoid drinking unfiltered tap water largely because I dislike the taste. Typically I drink filtered water and use a refillable, polycarbonate water bottle that does not contain the chemical bisphenol A, which is reportedly harmful to humans. However, I know many people who drink tap water with no apparent adverse effects.

Weight Management

According to news reports from numerous sources, the population in many industrialized countries keeps getting fatter. One reason for the increase in obesity may be that people are not getting adequate nutrition from the foods they eat. In an effort to obtain needed nutrients, their brains keep sending messages that prompt them to eat more. Yet even people who eat a seemingly balanced diet of nutritious foods in reasonable quantities may tend to be overweight if those foods do not contain enough life force energy. Processed foods, factory-farmed meat, and fruits and vegetables picked too early are lacking in life force energy and do not truly provide nourishment. The overweight person's body thinks it is starving and adjusts to compensate, storing more calories as fat. This phenomenon may hold true even if the person consumes a moderate quantity of food and does not overeat. Conversely, when the body is given fresh food that was raised naturally and contains life force energy, it knows it has been truly fed and maintains an appropriate weight.

In affluent societies where food is plentiful, it generally is considered desirable to be thin and undesirable to be heavy. While obesity is unhealthy and detracts from the quality of life, there is a larger range of acceptable weights than is presently recognized. A significant factor influencing body weight is personality and expression of energy. A person with a larger-than-life personality is likely to have a larger-than-average body. Conversely, extreme thinness may be a manifestation of a belief that one does not have the right to take up space in the world. For many people, it is natural and healthy to weigh more than the recommended figures on weight charts. If a person feels good and is happy with her body, there is no reason to force herself to fit the mold of what is currently fashionable.

In many cases, however, being overweight significantly detracts from health and enjoyment of life. Rather than trying one diet after the next, it makes sense to address the issue from a deeper level. As with age-related degeneration, body weight is inextricably linked to beliefs. Someone who believes he is inherently an overweight person is unlikely to be thin long-term. If you have a weight problem, rather than following the latest diet fad, pay attention to your feelings, thoughts, and actions, which reveal your underlying beliefs. Once you are aware of these beliefs and their influences, you can make a conscious choice of whether to continue to align with them.

Common reasons for being overweight include the need for protection and security. Some folks store too much fat for much the same reasons others hoard money: a fear of future scarcity. Those hoarding money may live a lifestyle of near-poverty, wearing old clothes, eating only inexpensive food, and avoiding spending for entertainment or vacations. They choose to live this way rather than dipping into their savings. Likewise, an overweight person may be chronically fatigued, yet unable to access the wealth of energy stored in his fat cells. In both cases, the underlying cause is a feeling of lack and fear of future scarcity. If, however, the money hoarder has an increase in income and feels secure that it will continue, he may be more willing to loosen up and use some of his riches. In a similar manner, if the overweight person starts giving his body the nutrients it needs, the body may start using the accumulated fat stores.

Chapter 9

Personal Care Without a Product Line

~~~

Anyone who keeps the ability to see beauty never grows old.
—Franz Kafka (European writer, 1883–1924)

Skin Care

My philosophy for personal care and beauty routines is to do the least you can to look the best you can, both short- and long-term. Spend your time and money on the practices and products that have a significant positive effect, and eliminate the rest.

In my experience, complicated and expensive skin care routines have not lived up to their claims. I still try new products occasionally, but have not found any that have made a significant difference in my skin. Rather than spending a fortune on the latest "miracle" cream, start reading labels to find products that do not contain ingredients that are likely to be irritating. In addition, I suggest avoiding products that blatantly claim to be anti-aging or wrinkle reducing. Every time you see the label, it will make you think you *need* to use something to fight aging and wrinkles.

Substances applied to the skin are absorbed into the body, so it is best not to apply anything to your skin that you would not put in your mouth. Common chemicals to avoid are sodium lauryl and laureth sulfates and ammonium lauryl and laureth sulfates (detergents present in many skin cleansers, liquid soaps, shampoos, and toothpastes), which severely dehydrate the skin and have been linked to a host of problems including eye irritation and canker sores. Propylene glycol, a humectant used in moisturizers, deodorants, and other personal care products, is the main ingredient in antifreeze. It can cause skin and eye irritation, damage skin and muscle tissue, and inhibit skin cell growth. Isopropyl alcohol, often listed on product labels as special denatured (SD) alcohol, also should be avoided. It is denatured is to keep people from drinking it, and the body treats it as a poison. Grain alcohol (the kind you can drink) is nontoxic and works well as a skin sanitizer and household disinfectant, although it is very drying when applied directly to the skin in undiluted form.

The best option for cleansing both skin and hair is a cleanser or shampoo that does not contain the aforementioned undesirable ingredients. (Natural foods stores carry this type of product.) You do not necessarily need different cleansers for various parts of the body. I used shampoo as an all-over cleanser long before body shampoos came into vogue; the ingredients are very similar. There also are cleansers and soaps in bar form that can be used on both the skin and hair.

In moisturizers, look for those that contain primarily natural oils (such as almond, apricot, avocado, coconut, jojoba, or olive), sometimes with natural waxes added to provide more staying power. An excellent all-over moisturizer is coconut oil (the organic kind used for cooking, not the cheaper coconut butter that is marketed as a cosmetic). Coconut oil has a melting point of about 25°C (76°F), so it is solid at room temperature in cooler climates. It works well as a moisturizer for the face, body, hands, and feet, and is excellent for conditioning hair. All this and it is good to eat as well! Coconut oil contains medium-chain fatty acids, which help support a healthy heart, immune system, and metabolism.

Facial Tapping

Facial tapping is a technique for stimulating acupressure points and improving circulation. I first used it when I was applying a moisturizer and felt compelled to start tapping briskly all over my face and head with the tips of my fingers. I tapped for a couple of minutes and observed that my skin looked firmer and more vibrant. After a few weeks of tapping daily, the effects were more noticeable. Several months later, I discovered that my facial tapping method is similar to *tapotement*, a massage technique that involves using the fingertips to lightly tap areas of the face or body.

The instructions for facial tapping are simple. With the fingertips (not the nails) of both hands, tap firmly enough to feel a "bounce," but not hard enough to cause pain. Tap all over the face and head for about two minutes. Perform facial tapping once or twice a day; after cleansing is a convenient time. Following is a suggested procedure. (There is no magic to this sequence; the best method is to follow your instincts and tap where – and for how long – it feels right.)

1) Tap the top of the cheekbones, moving outward and upward toward the temples.

2) Tap inward to the forehead, just above the eyebrows.

3) Tap along the brow bone, starting from the inner corner and moving in a circle around the eye socket, ending up at the nose bridge (avoid the eyeballs).

4) Tap lightly down the bridge and sides of the nose.

5) Tap across the cheeks, moving down to the jaw.

6) Tap along the jawbone, moving inward to the chin.

7) Tap the chin and all around the mouth.

8) Pull the lips gently over the teeth, and tap the lips.

9) With hand flat and fingers together, tap under the chin.

10) Move up to the center of the forehead, and tap outward and upward to the head.

11) Tap along the hairline and move outward and back, tapping all over the head and the back of the neck.

You can add an extra step to help stimulate the thymus gland (the master gland of the immune system), which is located behind the breastbone. Using the knuckles or fingertips of one hand, tap about 20 times in the middle of the upper chest, about four fingers' width below the V-shaped notch at the bottom of the neck. If you are ill or feel your immune system needs a boost, tap this area longer. The thymus tap can be repeated several times a day.

Facial Acupuncture and Acupressure

Acupuncture and acupressure techniques can help tone and firm facial contours and reduce wrinkles. Many acupuncturists offer facial rejuvenation acupuncture (also known as cosmetic acupuncture), which is defined as "the use of acupuncture techniques to revitalize facial skin tone and texture; reduce fine lines, wrinkles, puffiness, and loss of elasticity; and improve overall facial appearance." One acupuncturist told me he became interested in learning the rejuvenation techniques when one of his patients, a woman in her fifties whom he was treating for back pain, started receiving compliments from acquaintances who noticed she was looking younger.

While results are not as dramatic as with cosmetic surgery, facial rejuvenation acupuncture can yield visible improvements, especially if you continue to stimulate the acupuncture points yourself in a maintenance program. The book *Body Reflexology* contains complete instructions and diagrams for performing an "acupressure facelift."[28] Cosmetic acupuncture and acupressure not only pose no health risks, the treatments can have positive "side effects."

Facial Exercises

Facial exercises can enhance facial firmness and elasticity, improve contour, reduce lines; and revitalize skin color and tone. The idea that facial exercises cause wrinkles is a myth.

While repeatedly making the same facial expressions (which involves only partial extension and contraction of certain muscles) can lead to the formation of lines, properly performed facial exercises do not. Exercising the face strengthens muscles and helps rejuvenate the tissues by increasing blood circulation and energy flow.

There are numerous facial exercise programs; I will mention two effective ones. Facercise® is detailed in the book, *Carole Maggio Facercise®: The Dynamic Muscle-Toning Program for Renewed Vitality and a More Youthful Appearance.*[29] Carole Maggio, an aesthetician, began developing the exercises for herself in the early 1980s and has taught them to hundreds of thousands of clients.

FlexEffect® facial resistance training was developed by Deborah Crowley, a former competitive bodybuilder who applied the principles of bodybuilding to facial development and began teaching facial fitness in 1979. For more information on the program, see the FlexEffect website (flexeffect.com) or call 707-442-1166 or 800-879-9845 (toll-free).

Botox®

On the subject of facial movement, I would like to mention that I am not a fan of Botox (botulinum toxin injected into the face to paralyze muscles for cosmetic purposes) for three reasons. The first is that having a deadly poison injected near the eyes and brain – not just once, but repeatedly for years – strikes me as a bad idea. The long-term effects of such treatments are not yet known, and logic tells me that repeatedly poisoning oneself would have a detrimental effect on the entire body. If nothing else, the injection of the toxin likely causes a spike in free radical production, accelerating cell damage throughout the body. The second reason is that paralyzing muscles can cause atrophy of facial tissue, leading to the loss of facial tone – and sagging is even less attractive than expression lines. Thirdly, the use of Botox involves animal cruelty. Botulism toxin is so dangerous that each batch of the substance must be tested on animals to determine the proper dosage for use on humans. The animals that receive too much of the poison suffer an excruciating death.

In addition to these reasons for avoiding Botox, the bizarre "frozen face" effect seen in many of its users is neither attractive nor youthful looking. While I have never been accused of lacking vanity, having a deadly poison injected into my face and contributing to cruelty to living creatures would be going way over the top, particularly when the benefits of the treatments are a temporary fix that is likely to have detrimental health and beauty consequences long-term.

Skin Brushing

Dry brushing of the body is a health spa-inspired technique that removes dead skin cells, stimulates blood and lymph circulation, detoxifies the body, and reduces cellulite. Before each bath or shower, massage your entire body with a natural (plant-derived) bristle brush, sisal scrubber, or loofah sponge, and do *not* get it wet. Start with the soles of the feet, moving up each leg in circular motions or long strokes, and then massage the hips, buttocks, and torso up to the chest. Massage each hand and arm, and then massage the shoulders, neck, and chest. (Be gentle in delicate areas such as the neck and chest, and avoid the nipples.) Use a strap, large cloth, or long-handled brush to massage the back. Once a week, rinse the brush or scrubber with water and let it dry before the next use. In addition to the health benefits, dry brushing largely eliminates the need for applying moisturizer to the body.

Cold Water

Washing or rinsing with cold water helps stimulate circulation and tone the muscles that support the skin. For the face, avoid alternating exposure to very hot and cold water, as this can break capillaries. For the body, however, a warm shower followed by a cold rinse is beneficial. A cold rinse also is good for the hair and scalp. After a warm shower, I turn the water to a cold setting for as long as I can stand it, typically about 30 seconds. (If you try this, be careful! The first couple of times I stood under an ice-cold shower spray, it was such a shock to my system that I almost fainted.)

Sun Exposure

The issue of sun exposure and its effect on skin is paradoxical. The sun is necessary for life and health; how could it be harmful to us? Nevertheless, a quick look at the complexions of most people indicates that sun exposure causes damage to unprotected skin. More accurately, it shows that our culture has a strong belief that sun damages skin; therefore it does. There are, however, individuals who do not align with this belief and regularly expose their unprotected skin to the sun without adverse effects.

Many people *think* they believe that sun exposure is good for their skin, but this is not their actual belief. A simple way to discover your beliefs about sun exposure is to compare a frequently exposed area (such as your face or hands) to an area that is rarely exposed. If the less exposed area is in better condition than the more exposed area, obviously you believe sun exposure is detrimental to your skin! (This test may not be reliable for people under 30, since many of our beliefs about aging do not become apparent until later in life.) In addition, some of the skin damage blamed on sunlight may be due to exposure to fluorescent lighting, which can adversely affect the skin.

Nutrition also plays a role. There is some evidence that consuming unhealthy fats (hydrogenated, partially hydrogenated, or rancid oils) increases damage in skin exposed to ultraviolet light. Conversely, people with a high intake of EFAs and antioxidants generally experience less sun damage than those with unhealthy diets.

As with beliefs about toxic substances, the belief that exposure to ultraviolet light (from both natural and artificial sources) causes damage to unprotected skin is deeply ingrained in our culture. This is an area where I find it easier to go along with what I believe rather than try to convince myself otherwise. In my experience, consistent use of zinc oxide sunscreens has maintained (even improved) the condition and appearance of my skin.

Benefits of Sunlight

Although the sun apparently causes detrimental changes in unprotected skin, *some* direct sun exposure is beneficial and necessary for our health. (For example, sunlight reacts with skin oils to produce vitamin D.) The optimal areas for direct exposure may be the backs of the knees and insides of the elbows, where the skin is thin and blood vessels are close to the surface. The face, neck, and hands tend to be overexposed to the sun so much that I do not recommend leaving them unprotected. A better option is to have some direct sun exposure periodically on the legs and/or arms. Those who do not have frequent sun exposure on bare skin should make sure they eat a diet rich in vitamin D or take a supplement of vitamin D_3 (cholecalciferol), the most easily absorbed form.

For optimum health, we also need to be exposed to the full spectrum of natural light through our eyes.[30] Corrective lenses and window glass block some of these rays. For those who spend most of the day indoors, wearing ultraviolet-blocking sunglasses every time they are in direct sunlight is generally not a good practice. When dark glasses are worn, the pupils dilate to adjust to the darkness. When the glasses are removed, the eye suddenly is exposed to bright light when it is least able to deal with it. Indoor types might do well to limit the use of sunglasses to times when they are in intense sunlight for an extended period or are driving in bright sunshine. A good guideline to follow is that if you need to squint due to the sun's brightness or glare, shade your eyes with a hat, visor, or sunglasses.

Selecting a Sunscreen

The best sunscreens are mineral-based, with micronized (ground into tiny particles) zinc oxide as the active ingredient and no chemical sunscreens added. Zinc oxide blocks the broadest spectrum of ultraviolet A (UVA) and ultraviolet B (UVB) rays, as well as infrared rays, which also may damage the skin. UVB rays have their greatest effect on the epidermis (the outer, protective layer of the skin) and are mostly responsible for burning, tanning, hyperpigmentation (dark spots), and basal cell carcinoma (the most common and least serious form of skin cancer). UVA rays are longer and penetrate more deeply, causing damage to the dermis (the lower, connective tissue layer of the skin) that ultimately can result in loss of elasticity and other changes associated with aging. Another reason I prefer zinc oxide is that it does not have the irritation potential of chemical sunscreens. When applied to the skin, products with micronized zinc oxide do not have the stark white look characteristic of the original zinc oxide sunscreens.

Another commonly used mineral sunscreen is titanium dioxide, which is the active ingredient in many sunscreens labeled *mineral* or *nonchemical*. However, titanium dioxide blocks only part of the spectrum of UVA rays, so it is not as effective as zinc oxide. It also is more visible (ashy looking) on the skin. In addition, I prefer zinc (an essential nutrient) because it is more natural to the body than titanium.

My preference is for mineral-based sunscreens that contain at least 10 percent micronized zinc oxide and no chemical sunscreens. Contrary to common belief, the Sun Protection Factor (SPF) of a sunscreen product is not of paramount importance. SPF measures only the sunscreen's ability to block UVB (not UVA) rays. Some products with micronized zinc oxide as the only sunscreen ingredient have an SPF of 15 or less, yet they provide substantially more UVA protection than many of the chemical-containing sunscreens that are labeled SPF 30 or higher. Most products with a very high SPF have a high level of potentially irritating chemical sunscreens. When I used chemical sunscreens, I noticed that many of these products caused my skin to feel irritated when it was exposed to sunlight. The much-touted UVA sunscreen avobenzone (Parsol 1789) breaks down rapidly when exposed to ultraviolet light and can lose most of its potency in as little as one hour of sun exposure.

For sun protection for lips, thicker sunscreens that contain a substantial amount of oil or wax (for staying power) work well. In addition, some natural foods stores carry lip balms made of plant oils and waxes that contain micronized zinc oxide. If you wear lip color, you can apply a light layer of sunscreen to your lips before applying the lip color. A full-coverage lipstick provides some sun protection (at least an SPF 4) even if it does not contain sunscreen.

Hair Care

As with skin cleansers, avoid shampoos that contain sulfates or propylene glycol. If you use a shampoo without these chemicals, you may not need a hair conditioner. You can moisturize dry hair (typically the ends rather than the scalp) by applying a small amount of natural oil (such as almond, apricot, avocado, coconut, jojoba, or olive) prior to shampooing. Leave the oil on for 30 to 60 minutes and then wash your hair.

Blow dryers and other heated appliances can damage hair, especially if used frequently. Blow dryers also expose the user to high levels of electromagnetic frequencies, which is not a particularly good thing to blast your brain with. Try drying your hair naturally instead.

Acupressure methods can benefit the hair and scalp. A technique called *nail buffing* can help stimulate hair growth on the head. To perform nail buffing, place the four fingernails of one hand (leave out the thumb) against the four fingernails of the other hand, and rub them together briskly for at least 60 seconds. In addition to enhancing the hair, nail buffing is said to increase energy levels throughout the body.[31]

Dental Care

The only dental care products necessary for most people are dental floss and a toothbrush with soft, end-rounded, polished bristles. Dental tape and thicker types of dental floss tend to remove more plaque than thinner floss.

If you use toothpaste, choose a formula that is low in abrasion and does not contain fluoride. There is a great deal of controversy about the practice of adding fluoride to public water supplies and dental products. Excessive intake of fluoride can damage developing teeth (a condition known as *dental fluorosis*) and adversely affect the bones and other body systems. Keep in mind that fluoride is present not just in dental products and drinking water, but also in soft drinks, juices, and canned and frozen foods.

Dental Services

Dentists are the only health professionals I have visited on a consistent basis. However, I know people with healthy teeth and gums who have not been to a dentist in years. If you use dental services, it is imperative to find a dentist that is highly skilled and knowledgeable about overall health. Inappropriate dental work can cause a myriad of problems throughout the body. When choosing a dentist, I rule out those that still use amalgam (silver) fillings, even if they offer alternatives. Amalgam contains mercury, and someone who would put a toxic substance like mercury into a person's mouth cannot be trusted with health-related decisions! In addition, I favor dentists with a conservative approach to dental work in general. For instance, a small cavity that is no longer actively decaying may not need to be drilled and filled.

Like the rest of the body, teeth and gums are affected by a person's beliefs and intentions. I am aware of at least two cases in which individuals were told they needed extensive dental work but corrected the problems themselves with their intention and belief they could do so. They went back to the dentist a few months later and were told they no longer needed the previously recommended procedures. This is yet another area in which we are limited only by our beliefs of what is possible. Teeth are living structures that can regenerate.

Oil Pulling

Oil pulling is a holistic remedy developed in India that is intended to detoxify the mouth and body by removing mucous, bacteria, and toxins from the body through the saliva. There are scores of anecdotal reports about health benefits derived from this practice. I cannot personally attest to the accuracy of these reports, but have used the technique and found that it helped alleviate dental problems and whitened my teeth. For tooth whitening, oil pulling is healthier and less expensive than bleaching.

Here are basic instructions for oil pulling: After you wake up in the morning, on an empty stomach (before eating, drinking, or brushing your teeth), take one tablespoon of cold-pressed vegetable oil into your mouth. Slowly swish, suck, and pull the oil through the teeth for about 15 to 20 minutes. Do not swallow the oil or gargle with it (but if you accidentally swallow some oil, it won't hurt you.) By the time you spit it out, the oil should be thoroughly mixed with saliva into thin, white foam. (If it is still yellow, you haven't pulled it long enough.) Spit the oil into the toilet, rinse your mouth thoroughly with water, and drink a glass of pure water. It is recommended that oil pulling be performed daily, first thing in the morning. For faster detoxification it can be done one or two more times during the day, but always on an empty stomach.

There is some controversy regarding the types of vegetable oil used for oil pulling. Purists claim that sesame and sunflower oil yield the best results, but others have had good results with other types of cold-pressed oils such as coconut, olive, and safflower. Some people have found it beneficial to switch among different types of oils. Avoid using canola oil (in food as well as oil pulling) because it may have toxic properties.

Vision Care

The idea that once eyesight deteriorates, it cannot improve and must be "treated" with corrective lenses or surgery is false. Many people have improved their eyesight naturally and discarded corrective lenses. An excellent resource for accomplishing this type of change is the book, *Take Off Your Glasses and See: A Mind/Body Approach to Expanding Your Eyesight and Insight* by Jacob Liberman, OD, PhD.[32] I recommend this book even for people who do not have vision problems. Dr. Liberman's insights about the broader aspects of vision and eyesight are mind broadening, and they helped validate my lifelong choice to avoid eye doctor visits even when they were offered at no charge. (I have always instinctively known that subjecting myself to eye tests and checkups would not be beneficial. This is my personal choice and not a recommendation for others, but in my case it has worked well.)

The idea that vision always deteriorates with age also is not true. A man I know was told by an optometrist that everyone becomes farsighted at age 40. By the time he was 41, this man (who previously had excellent eyesight) was wearing reading glasses. Since I knew people in their forties and fifties who did not wear glasses, I realized this was not a valid or useful belief and consciously chose not to align with it.

Years later I went through a period when I noticed I needed a bit more light than usual when reading and that fine print looked a little blurry. Rather than concluding that I needed glasses, whenever I was having trouble reading, I looked away briefly, reminded myself that I could choose to see and read whatever I wanted to, and then looked back at the written material. When I looked the second time, I perceived the print clearly.

In the late 1800s and early 1900s, ophthalmologist William Bates, MD, developed techniques for improving eyesight that helped eliminate the need for corrective lenses in many individuals. An eye relaxation technique Bates recommended for everyone is called *palming*. To perform palming, cup your hands and place them over your closed eyes without putting pressure on the eyeballs or face. Relax the eye muscles, and preferably the rest of your body as well. The aim is to allow as little light as possible to enter the eye, so a darkened room is ideal. If you are lying down in a lighted room, put a towel or cloth over your hands to block more light. Palming at least once a day for five minutes or more is ideal (a good time is right before you go to sleep at night). Alternatively, you can take numerous mini-breaks throughout the day by palming for one minute or less.

Another way to help maintain acute vision is to avoid staring rigidly in the same position for an extended period. Move your eyes and head regularly. When you are reading, doing paperwork, or using a computer, look up every few minutes and briefly focus on something far away. Do not stare or strain; simply focus on the point for a moment or two. (For instance, read the title of a book on a shelf across the room.) Take short breaks from your work by alternately looking at objects that are far, very close, and a medium distance away. It also helps to focus alternately on things of contrasting colors.

Certain nutrients can help maintain vision and improve eye health. Lutein and zeaxanthin (antioxidants in the carotenoid family) are particularly good for the eyes. Both nutrients are present in high concentrations in kale, spinach, and other dark green leafy vegetables. Bilberries contain high levels of lutein.

Plastic Surgery

At some point our beliefs will be more in alignment with our desires, and most of us will choose not to manifest signs of age-related degeneration. Presently, this obviously is not the case. Like other medical treatments, plastic surgery can be used as a tool to make changes on a physical level that we have not yet been able to create by other means. This view is different from the approach of desperately attempting to hold onto youth by trying every new cosmetic procedure advertised. If you believe age-related degeneration is inevitable and are attempting to do everything possible to stave it off, then plastic surgery (like any other anti-aging technique) will be a stopgap measure at best.

I used to believe plastic surgery was the most effective kind of elective surgery, since (unlike many other types of operations) it typically left patients feeling better than they did before. I still feel this way about reconstructive surgery (for injuries and deformities); the marvels performed by good reconstructive surgeons are life transforming for their patients. But with the advent of "extreme makeover" contests and television shows, I have altered my views somewhat about cosmetic surgery. While it can be a wonderful tool, it is apparent that it is being used inappropriately. A glance at some of the celebrity before-and-after pictures on certain websites will raise one's eyebrows higher than a bad brow lift! In all seriousness, cosmetic surgery is not the answer to the aesthetic problems of aging. A person who believes strongly in the inevitability of degeneration and tries to fight it with cosmetic procedures is likely to end up looking like an old person who has had a lot of plastic surgery.

If you choose to have plastic surgery, here are some points to keep in mind:

- Choose an excellent surgeon, preferably one with extensive experience performing the procedure in which you are interested. Ask to see before-and-after pictures, and if possible, talk to some former patients. Above all, follow your intuition and feelings about whether a particular doctor is right for you. Good credentials and references are important, but do not let these override your instincts.

- The three most important words in plastic surgery are *communication, communication, communication!* It is of the utmost importance to clearly communicate your desired results to the doctor, and for the doctor to explain thoroughly what she thinks can be accomplished. In addition, make sure you understand the potential complications and requirements (including activity limitations) for the recovery period.

- Be cautious about having any substance injected or implanted into your face or body. Before making a decision to undergo this type of procedure, obtain as much information about the substance as you can. New compounds are continually being developed, and sometimes these materials have effects that do not become apparent until long after the procedure.

- Know when to quit. Sometimes when an individual has one or two cosmetic procedures and is happy with the result, he continues to have more plastic surgery. After a certain point, the person starts to look unnatural, possibly even ghoulish. The most successful cosmetic operations leave patients looking like themselves, only better.

Part Four:

Delving Deeper

Chapter 10

Streamlining and Simplifying

~~~

Our life is frittered away by detail... Simplify, simplify![33]
—Henry David Thoreau (American writer, 1817–1862)

Old Stuff Leads to Old Folks

How could hanging on to old stuff possibly have anything to do with aging? When you consider the energetic implications of holding onto things we no longer need, it is not so surprising that accumulating objects can be related to aging. Not letting go of physical items is a reflection of our unwillingness to release emotional issues and outworn ideas. When we retain these things in our energy field, they affect the physical body (which may help explain the slowdown in the body's metabolic processes that typically occurs as people age). If we want our bodies to start fresh with optimally functioning, undamaged cells, we must learn to start fresh and release things we are holding onto that no longer serve us.

Many people keep too much stuff largely out of fear – fear they will need it in the future or regret letting go of it for some other reason. Yet having too many possessions can sap your life force energy. Your life force is present in everything you own and all of your commitments. Do you truly want your energy to be dissipated into overflowing closets, a myriad of appliances, and memberships in organizations that no longer interest you?

In modern society, we have learned not to trust ourselves and to rely on outside means of verification. Many of our products (medications, nutritional supplements, and cosmetics) are props we have come to believe we need to use to maintain our physical bodies. Clocks, thermometers, scales, and other measurement and monitoring systems have taken the place of our own senses. When we learn to rely more on our innate capabilities, we may find we don't require so many material things. Remember that the less you use, the less you need.

Clutter and Excess Weight

Can clutter make you fat? As with aging, having too much stuff is related to being overweight. In both cases, a person has taken on (or in) more than they need or can use. One reason so many people are overweight may be that they are unwilling or afraid to let go of things they no longer need. Just as their closets, bureaus, and basements are stuffed with more possessions than they require, their body's storage areas are overfilled as well. When you alter your attitude and habits so that you acquire and use only the items you need, you can apply this awareness to your food choices and eating habits as well. Over time, without dieting, you will find that your weight adjusts to a healthier level.

Your Stuff and Your Identity

Clutter and complication are highly regarded in modern society. We are taught to assess ourselves by our productivity, which typically is equated with some kind of physical result. Often the value (and broad-ranging effects) of that result are not considered. As Henry David Thoreau observed, "If a man walks in the woods for love of them half of each day, he is in danger of being regarded as a loafer. But if he spends his days as a speculator, shearing off those woods and making the earth bald before her time, he is deemed an industrious and enterprising citizen."

Remember that you are more than what you own and what you do (the roles you play in daily life). If you lost your job and your savings, your house burned down, and all your belongings were destroyed, would you feel you had lost your identity? Perhaps one of the reasons many people are so afraid of dying is that they know they won't be able take any of their stuff with them, and they don't know who they would be without it. Your identity is intrinsic to your being; it does not depend on external factors or possessions.

If In Doubt, Throw It Out

From nearly every direction we are pressured to purchase products and services, to the point that our "stuff" has become overwhelming. I am not suggesting that everyone dispense with everything not required for survival; the point is to eliminate things that consume more energy than they provide. Once you do, you will have more time, energy, money, and space in your life for what truly is most fulfilling. Remember that the less stuff you own, the less you have to clean and maintain. To paraphrase Parkinson's Law (work expands to fill the time available for its completion), stuff expands to fill the space available to store it – and then some.

The concept of streamlining is not about denying yourself; it is about realizing you don't need so much. Purchasing just the right product or service is not the key to youth, health, success, happiness, or anything else. The true answers are inside yourself, and you will find them faster if you are not weighed down by possessions and overwhelmed with commitments.

Streamlining Suggestions

Here are some ideas for simplifying and streamlining:

- The basics of streamlining are to eliminate, simplify, and organize – in that order. When you implement organizing systems and methods, make them as simple as possible.

167

- Streamlining does not mean going back to basics and ignoring modern advances. Keep up with technological developments, new products, and fashion trends, but incorporate only those that appeal to you. When you add something new, discard the old version (don't just stuff it in the back of a closet).

- Consciously choose the objects, relationships, and commitments you want in your life. Eliminate anything that no longer is (or never was) important to you, including possessions, activities, and relationships. If you pare down in most areas, you have more resources available for the things that are most important and enjoyable to you now.

- An interest, hobby, or activity you enjoyed in the past may not be something you want to continue. Be honest with yourself and let it go. Sell or donate the equipment, collection, or other paraphernalia to someone who will benefit from it as you once did. Divesting yourself of what is no longer useful creates room (both literally and figuratively) in your life for new interests. Keep things (books, money, ideas) in circulation; do not hoard or hang onto what you no longer need.

- Get rid of anything that makes you feel bad when you look at or think about it. We have energetic associations with our possessions. Owning an object connects you to things you might not want to be connected to, such as a former spouse or a job you disliked. A ring from an old boyfriend does not just remind you of him; it energetically links you to him.

- When you are making a decision on something, an overarching question to ask is *Does this (object, activity, relationship) support the person I want to be?* If the answer is no, release it from your life.

- Before you buy an item, consider not only if it will serve your needs and is a reasonable price, but also how much complication it will engender. Think about the complications entailed by owning just one appliance or electronic device: you must file the instructions and warranty; purchase batteries or bulbs, and clean, repair, and possibly insure the item. Decide if the function it serves is important enough to offset the complications it creates.

- If you do not already use the Internet, consider doing so – it is a great streamlining tool. Having access to information in electronic form makes it unnecessary to keep reference books, phone directories, catalogs, magazines, reports, articles, letters, and other paper items. Think of all the trees that can be saved!

Clutter Traps

Memorabilia

Memorabilia (greeting cards, ticket stubs, sports trophies, photographs, and so forth) is the biggest clutter trap for many people, and one of the most challenging to deal with because emotions are involved. The best time to sort through your collection of mementos is when you are feeling happy, energetic, and confident. If a person, event, trip, or anything else was truly significant to you, you will remember it without having to save a lot of stuff as a reminder.

Sometimes people keep things out of habit that remind them of individuals or events they would just as soon not remember. There is not much point in saving pictures of the girlfriend who dumped you or the hood ornament from the car that was totaled in an accident that put you in the hospital for two weeks. Letting go of objects that trigger unpleasant memories helps free you of the emotional burden as well.

The most efficient way to manage memorabilia clutter is to accumulate as little as possible. When you take a vacation, aim to "get away from it all" without bringing more of it back. Pass up the overpriced, useless trinkets in souvenir shops in favor of functional items such as clothing. Also, it is not mandatory to bring a camera when you travel. In popular vacation areas, I often have noticed that some folks seem to pay more attention to taking photos than they do to actually experiencing the place they traveled to see. If you want to show friends and family pictures of the beautiful sights you saw, you can buy postcards. Your loved ones know what you look like, and no doubt they believe you were there. The professional photographers who shot the postcard photos probably did more justice to the Eiffel Tower or Grand Canyon than you will with your pocket camera. Without a camera weighing you down, you are more free to experience and enjoy the sights you traveled so far to see.

Gifts

Often the best kinds of gifts are those that do not last – that is, that do not produce clutter. Such gifts include event tickets, foods or beverages, gift cards, or personal service gift certificates (for services such as two hours of housecleaning or an automobile oil change). Flowers are a lovely gift because the recipient can enjoy them for a few days without having to find storage space as they would for a more permanent item.

To minimize the number of unwanted gifts you receive, inform friends and relatives that you are decluttering. Let them know that to celebrate special occasions, you would prefer to spend time with them (possibly at a theater, museum, or your favorite restaurant) rather than receive a conventional gift. Another suggestion is that they donate to your favorite charity the money they would have spent on a gift.

Books

Books you valued in the past may not represent who you are now. Go through all the books you own and sort them into three categories: books you use as references, those you truly want to read or reread, and those you do not want to read or reread and are unlikely to use as a reference. Be honest with yourself – if you think you should read a book but have no desire to, put it in the third pile. Immediately place the books in the third category in a box to donate or sell in the next few days.

If you feel bad about disposing of books, remember that the tomes collecting dust on your shelf could be bringing knowledge and enjoyment to others. Unread books not only clutter your living area, they can be a psychological drain as well. Every time you see or think about all the books you "should" read, you add more tasks to your mental to-do list. Giving away those guilt-producing books can take a load off your mind as well as off your shelves.

Use It or Lose It

For streamlining your living spaces, follow the advice of nineteenth century poet and decorator William Morris: "Have nothing in your houses that you do not know to be useful or believe to be beautiful."

Decluttering is most effective when done in stages. Review the items in a particular category, remove the ones you know you should discard, and make decisions on the "maybes." After you have finished evaluating all your possessions and disposing of the excess (a process that may take days, weeks, or months), take a break and enjoy the feelings of pride, satisfaction, and freedom you will have because of your efforts. When you feel like cleaning up again (and you will – decluttering can become addictive!), go back to the first areas you decluttered and reevaluate the items you kept. It is likely you will identify additional items you no longer want. Over time, review all the areas you decluttered. You may be surprised at how much more you can discard.

Decluttering Process

To prepare for the decluttering process, collect six large containers (boxes, bags, or wastebaskets). You will use these containers for items to be: (1) thrown away, (2) donated to charity or sold, (3) given or returned to other people, (4) cleaned or repaired, (5) moved to another location, and (6) decided on later. Make decisions as you go along, but if you truly are perplexed about something, put it in the sixth container rather than spending a lot of time on it. When evaluating your possessions, ask yourself the following questions.

- How do I feel about this item?

- How often do I use it?

- Do I have other items that serve the same purpose?

- If it were lost or destroyed, would I replace it?

- If not replaceable, would I truly miss it or be relieved that it was gone?

- What is the worst thing that could happen if I needed this item and did not have it?

First pare down to the things you actually use, and then evaluate those to see if you could manage with fewer items. For example, you may have five shampoos and nine types of ink pens. You might use each of them occasionally, but you probably do not need all those variations. If you want to keep more than one of a certain item, set a quantity limit. For example, allow yourself a maximum of two shampoos, four types of ink pens, and two pairs of athletic shoes. If you want to add another, eliminate one of the current ones.

For things you know you should discard but cannot bring yourself to part with just yet, use the following method: Pack the items in boxes or bags and put them in a storage area, preferably where you won't see them often. On your calendar, mark a date three months in the future. When the day of reckoning arrives, either go through the boxes again or (if you are brave) discard or donate them without looking at the contents. If you have not needed something in three months, you probably can live without it.

When you finally get rid of something you have been mulling over, you are free from having to make that decision ever again. Each time you think about an item and decide not to discard it, you know you will have to evaluate it again in the future.

Some people feel it is wasteful to give away an item that is still in good condition, but if you do not really need something that could be used by others, it is more wasteful to keep it. Many charitable organizations accept donations of useable items and will provide a receipt for income tax documentation. If you aren't aware of such an organization, search online or look under the Social Services listing in a phone directory. Some charities have a pickup service that will come to your home, which makes it easy to donate furniture and larger items.

Managing New Purchases

When decluttering, your motto should be, "If in doubt, throw it out." When shopping, however, if in doubt, leave it out (of the shopping cart). As with eating, it is best not to develop a habit of using shopping (whether at malls, boutiques, yard sales, or online) as a recreational activity. I can imagine the shopping center planners saying, "If we build them, they will spend."

To avoid recluttering your newly decluttered areas, be judicious about acquiring additional items. Before making a decision to purchase something, ask yourself the following questions:

- How will owning this improve my life?
- Do I already have something that serves the same purpose? If so, am I willing to discard the old one?
- Will the acquiring the item necessitate other purchases?
- Do I truly want this item or am I responding to advertisements, other people's expectations, or the force of habit?
- Would I be interested in buying this item if it was not on sale?
- Is the item described as a "collectible" or "collector's item"? (It may not say so in the dictionary, but these terms are synonyms for clutter.)
- Where will I put it and how much space will it take up?
- What type of maintenance, cleaning, and/or replaceable parts does this item require?
- Can I borrow or rent this item instead of buying it?
- For clothing and fashion accessories, is the item comfortable and a good fit?

If you don't truly need or want something, do not accept it just because someone offers it at no charge. You probably know that renting a storage facility is expensive, but the space used for storing things in your home also costs money (a portion of your mortgage or rent). The next time you are tempted to acquire something you don't need simply because it is offered for free or at a bargain price, think about how much it will cost you to store it. Think about what it is costing you to store the unnecessary things you already have.

Chapter 11

The Ultimate Taboo

~~~

Life is eternal, and love is immortal, and death is only a horizon, and a horizon is nothing save the limit of our sight.

—Rossiter W. Raymond (American writer, 1840–1918)

The Longevity Question

With even a cursory look at this book, it is apparent that I do not believe age-related degeneration is inevitable. Unlike many in the anti-aging camp, however, I have no interest in promoting the idea of physical immortality or even extreme longevity. It is likely that humans could routinely live well over 100 years if they wanted to and believed it was possible, but physical mortality is one of the "ground rules" or blueprints of this reality. While it is possible for an individual to move outside these blueprints, it is not something I personally aspire to do in the area of lifespan.

There are scientists and physicians who postulate that by 2050, technology will exist to extend the human lifespan indefinitely. Their strategy is to use health practices (lifestyle changes, nutritional supplements, and other therapies) to ensure they are still alive when the technological breakthroughs occur. My view is that by 2050, our comprehension of the multidimensional natural of reality will be such that few people will be motivated to live forever in their current physical body. As souls we are immortal. Existing in the same body eternally would be as limiting as choosing to reside in the same location forever! If you truly believe that more exists than what we experience in this physical dimension, then what is the point of striving for physical immortality?

Personally I have no desire for extreme longevity, and since childhood have known I will not reach an advanced age. When I have experienced close calls in which I could have been killed or seriously injured, afterwards I felt a great appreciation – almost a feeling of euphoria – for being alive and healthy, which is something I take for granted most of the time. Yet I am not particularly afraid of death (except for fears about dying in an uncomfortable way) and have no doubt that I will continue to exist afterward.

It has been suggested that perhaps I do not want to live to an old age so I can avoid the degeneration most people believe is inevitable, but that is not the reason. Even with a perennially youthful body and brain (which is something we all have the ability to create), I still would choose not to live to an advanced age. At some point well before the 100-year mark, I expect I will feel I have had enough experience in this realm and want to move on.

An Alternative View of Death

Ironically, with the many authentic phenomena that our mainstream culture fails to acknowledge (telepathy, clairvoyance, energy healing, and so forth), some things almost universally accepted as genuine are invalid. Prominent among these false concepts is our idea of death: the belief that a conscious personality can truly cease to exist. The human body can be destroyed, but consciousness cannot be extinguished – it merely changes form. If we understood this concept, we would be much more accepting of a person's choice to pass on. Yes, it is a choice: every individual who leaves physical life has chosen to do so, although he may not be consciously aware of this choice prior to disengaging.

In our culture death is viewed not as a choice, but as a failure: the doctors failed to save the patient and the patient failed to survive. We often hear people make statements like, "He lost his battle with cancer." In many cases, individuals who are ready to die prolong their suffering because they know their loved ones are not ready to let go. It would serve us well to learn to accept death as a natural stage of life rather than viewing it as something to be feared and conquered.

Some individuals already have this attitude. When they feel it is time to move on from this world, they simply go into a meditative state and quietly leave their body. This practice is common enough among advanced yoga masters in India that there is a word for it: *mahasamadhi*. This apparent "voluntary death" is almost incomprehensible to many Westerners, but it seems a much better choice than suffering with illness or trauma.

Given our cultural attitudes about death, the following idea may seem appalling, but I am suggesting it anyway. Rather than trying to keep people alive at all costs, we could accept that we are going to die and plan for it. (This idea isn't much different from what happens when employees give notice before they leave a job and their coworkers arrange a going-away celebration.) As it typically is done now, friends and family gather only after their loved one has passed on. In cases where a person knows she has a limited amount of time left, it would make more sense to have everyone gather while she is still alive. Rather than just reminiscing about the person after she has passed on, they could enjoy interacting with her while she is still here physically.

The Mystery of Life After Death

Many people fear death largely because they don't know what to expect when it occurs. Regardless of our religious or philosophical beliefs, most of us feel clueless about what happens to people when they leave this realm. I expect that dying will be a lot like waking up from a dream: I will experience much greater clarity and be relieved to find that the problems and situations I have been struggling with are not "real." The idea that nothing exists beyond this physical life is as ludicrous to me as the idea that nothing exists outside the building I am in now. I may not be able to physically see anything else at the moment, but that does not mean it isn't there.

The numerous accounts of near-death experiences support the fact that there is life after death, but they do not necessarily provide an accurate description of what may happen to each of us when we pass on. I believe near-death experiences are very real; they are not hallucinations any more than our daily waking life is a hallucination. These experiences are, however, heavily influenced by a person's beliefs and expectations about what happens after death. A Christian may see angels or Jesus, for instance, while a Hindu may encounter the god Brahma or the goddess Lakshmi. Near-death experiences differ from actual death in a fundamental way: the person returns to our physical reality. I consider near-death experiences to be like field trips to another realm. The first few minutes after death do not reveal what the afterlife is truly like any more than the first few minutes after birth give an accurate idea of what physical life is like.

After decades of metaphysical study, I have come to understand that what people experience after physical death is based upon the beliefs they hold in life. Therefore, individuals' after-death experiences can vary greatly. While I do not believe there is a heaven or hell as depicted in religious belief systems, someone who believes in the existence of heaven can actually create such a place, complete with winged angels floating on clouds. A person with similar beliefs who feels he has lived an evil life may create a fiery hell populated with suffering sinners and pitchfork-wielding devils. Fortunately these creations are temporary; eventually the person moves past these beliefs.

Messages from those who have passed on (communicated through professional mediums and numerous personal accounts) almost overwhelmingly indicate that people are happier in the afterlife than they were in their physical lives. I once visited a psychic reader who knew immediately (without my giving her any information) that one of my relatives had died within the past month. She told me she sensed that the woman was pointing to her head and chest (the areas where she had cancer) and saying, "If I had known how it would be here [in the afterlife], I wouldn't have fought [death] so hard." In two other instances, friends have told me of experiences in which they were extremely distraught over a loved one's passing, and the departed person actually paid them a visit. In neither case did the person speak, but they looked so joyful and radiant that there was no doubt they were happy in their new environment.

Continuing Communication

Many people who suspend their disbelief in the possibility of communication with individuals who have departed this realm find they can continue the relationship, albeit in an altered form. Such communication can be accomplished through another person (a medium), but there are other methods as well. Direct interaction with those "on the other side" may occur in dreams and can be achieved through intention and focus while in a relaxed, meditative state. Simply opening yourself to these types of experiences (and paying attention throughout the day) will allow you to notice communications that may come in subtle ways. For instance, you may be thinking about the person, wondering how he is doing in his new environment, and then you turn on the radio and hear a song that gives you the answer. Communications of this type can come from virtually any source: people, animals, birds, plants, music, books, movies, and the Internet, in addition to your own feelings and impressions.

The potential for communication after physical death can perhaps best be illustrated by an analogy. A woman I know named Anne, well loved by her many friends and family members, passed on after a long struggle with cancer. She maintained her optimistic disposition even in the worst of times and is deeply missed by her loved ones. Rather than believing that Anne is "dead and gone," I view the situation much as if she relocated from her home in Virginia to a distant country. She loved being near her family and friends, but the climate and conditions in Virginia did not agree with her any longer. In her new home, she has regained her health and feels good again. It has been a long time since Anne visited the place, so there is much for her to explore in that beautiful country, as well as many old friends she wants to catch up with.

While Anne will miss her loved ones in the United States (and it will be quite awhile before she sees most of them face-to-face again), they can keep in touch with her via phone calls, email, letters, and other means of communication. To accomplish this, however, her friends and family must acknowledge two things: that Anne is still alive, and that it is possible to communicate with her. They may not be able to establish communication immediately, as it may take some time for Anne to get her bearings in her new home. In addition, the view from her new vantage point is much broader. Her awareness encompasses a great deal more than it did prior to her passing; therefore her attention is likely to be focused in areas other than our physical world. Eventually, however, she may make contact, especially if she senses people would like to hear from her.

For this system to work, however, Anne's loved ones must establish phone service, create an email account, or put up a mailbox – and they need to check for messages regularly. If they do not believe Anne's personality is still alive and accessible from our physical world, these avenues of communication remain closed to them. The real tragedy here is not Anne's passing, but our failure to recognize the true nature of physical death: that it is a transition rather than an ending, and that Anne can still be in our lives.

This story sounds wonderful, you may be thinking, but has anyone (other than a few famous mediums) ever accomplished this sort of thing? The answer is yes – many people have done so, including several I have known. For example, Jeanette, a friend I used to work with, communicated with her father in the dream state for several years after he passed on. On a regular basis, she had dreams in which she was talking with her father. Often he would give her helpful advice on situations she was dealing with.

The last year of Jeanette's father's life coincided with the first year of her son's life, and one of her father's greatest joys was spending time with the baby. It was virtually the only time he was not in pain from cancer. One night a couple of months after his death, Jeanette was in distress over the baby's incessant crying. She had gotten up numerous times to attend to her son, but nothing she did soothed him for long. Sleep-deprived and frustrated, Jeanette was losing her ability to cope with the situation. Once again the child started screaming, so she got out of bed and went to in his room. When she walked in the door, Jeanette was dumbfounded. Not only had the baby stopped crying, he was smiling and giggling softly. Her son was looking upward and acting as if someone were standing over the crib, playing with him! The scene was eerily familiar to Jeanette. It was as if, once again, her father was playing with his beloved grandson. She watched for a couple of minutes, and then returned to her room without disturbing the child. He was quiet for the rest of the night.

It often is easier for small children to communicate with the departed simply because they have not yet learned that it is not supposed to be possible. A colleague once told me that his four-year-old daughter said she regularly talked with her deceased great-grandmother. One time he saw the little girl alone in her room, apparently having a conversation with someone he could not see. The family had been worried about his wife's mother, who was in the hospital recovering from surgery. The little girl came bouncing out of her room, ecstatic because her great-grandmother had just told her, "Grandma is going to be fine." And indeed she was.

Regarding intentional communication with those who have passed on, keep in mind that they may not contact us every time we want them to. After physical death, people do not become static and remain just as you remembered them. Their awareness is much broader, and they grow and change with their new experiences. Much like a teenager who goes away to college, they may be so caught up in their new experiences that they forget to "answer our calls." It does not mean they don't care about us; it simply means their attention is focused elsewhere. Also (to continue my earlier analogy), sometimes the phone connection is interrupted or there is atmospheric interference. The dream state often is the easiest avenue for those who have passed on to make contact with us, as we generally are more receptive then.

The fundamental point to remember is that when loved ones leave their physical bodies, nothing has been lost – they are alive as they ever were, and the connection you share with them is eternal.

A Broader Perspective

My friend Justin told me about a significant dream he had, and I often think of it. The setting was a huge party in the afterlife. Justin was there with everyone he had ever known, everyone *they* had ever known, and so on. All the people were having a great time, talking and laughing about who had done what to whom. It was much like a cast party after a stage play, when the person who played the murderer is joyfully sharing a meal with the "victim." Both actors know that what happened in the play does not really make any difference. Beneath the costumes and makeup, they are good friends who care deeply about one another.

Justin's dream struck me as profound. It is a great illustration of the way I believe things truly are, once we transcend our beliefs in right versus wrong and good versus evil. In our daily dramas, each of us simply plays our role. In the greater scheme of things, no one ever dies.

Afterword

From my personal experience, I advise people not to be disappointed if they don't notice immediate and dramatic physical changes when they start incorporating these ideas. Certainly it is possible to undergo an abrupt alteration (and I do not want to discourage anyone from accomplishing that), but with longstanding, deeply rooted beliefs, there usually is a more gradual shift. The new ideas begin infiltrating your consciousness and the more you reinforce them, the stronger they become. The less you reinforce the old beliefs (by thinking and talking about getting old, worrying about age-associated disorders, and so forth), the sooner they fade away.

Once you recognize that an idea is a belief rather than an absolute truth, it gives you the freedom to choose whether you want to hold that belief and be subject to its "rules." When we recognize that most age-related degeneration is due to our beliefs, we can make the choice not to align with those beliefs. It really is that simple.

It is best to avoid monitoring yourself for physical signs of aging or youthfulness, which tends to make you focus on (and perpetuate) the characteristics you dislike. Instead, let the positive changes sneak up on you. A year from now, you may see an old photo of yourself and realize you look younger than you did then. Perhaps you will notice that some physical problems have disappeared or that your mental sharpness has returned. As your beliefs shift over time, you will find that your experience of aging differs more and more from the experiences of your contemporaries.

Applying these ideas has made a significant difference in my experience of aging. From my early twenties to mid-thirties (when I held conventional beliefs about aging), people typically assumed I was several years older than my chronological age. Now this trend has reversed, and people often assume I am younger than my age. In addition, I have not noticed a decline in physical or mental functioning, nor have I developed age-related conditions or diseases.

In the past, when I noticed physical signs of aging in myself or someone else, I thought of them as a natural consequence of growing older. Now I consider such signs to be evidence that the person aligns with the belief that the body degenerates with age. Viewed in that manner, physical indications of aging are helpful communications about the state of one's beliefs. In addition, I no longer consider age-related changes to be permanent conditions that will worsen over time. I expect my body to change as my beliefs change, which means I may well start looking younger.

You now have the knowledge that your existence does not have to be a downward spiral from the peak of young adulthood to a dismal old age. When you think about aging and health, above all, remember that your physical body is a manifestation of what you create through your beliefs and choices. Our DNA does not dictate our destiny – we have the power to change anything in our experience. As long as you are alive, you possess the ability to truly *live*.

~~~

Since everything is but an apparition, perfect in being what it is, having nothing to do with good or bad, acceptance or rejection, one may well burst out in laughter.

—Longchenpa (Tibetan Buddhist teacher, 1308–1364)

Notes

1 Bruce Lipton, PhD, "The Biology of Belief" (2001), http://www.brucelipton.com.

2 Lipton.

3 Lipton.

4 Osamu Nishikaze, PhD, University of Hokkaido, Japan.

5 Bruce Lipton, PhD, *The Biology of Belief: Unleashing the Power of Consciousness, Matter, and Miracles* (Santa Cruz, CA: Mountain of Love, 2005).

6 Michael Talbot, *The Holographic Universe* (New York, NY: Harper Perennial, 1992), pp. 87-88.

7 Stephen Hawley Martin, *Past Fear and Doubt to Amazing Abundance: Secret Knowledge That Brought Me Self-Actualization* (Richmond, VA: Oaklea Press, 2000), pp. 9-10.

8 Robert M. Williams, MA, *PSYCH-K: The Missing Peace in Your Life!* (Crestone, CO: Myrddin Publications, 2004), pp. 115-117.

9 Alan Cohen, *I Had It All the Time: When Self-Improvement Gives Way to Ecstasy* (Makawao, HI: Alan Cohen Publications, 1994), pp. 230-231.

10 Bob Dylan, *My Back Pages* (Warner Bros., 1964 and Special Rider Music, 1992).

11 Talbot, pp. 98-99.

[12] J. L. Glaser, J. L. Brind, J. H. Vogelman, M. J. Eisner, M. C. Dillbeck, R. K. Wallace, D. Chopra, and N. Orentreich, "Elevated serum dehydroepiandrosterone sulfate levels in practitioners of the Transcendental Meditation (TM) and TM-Sidhi programs," Journal of Behavioral Medicine, 1992, Vol. 15(4), pp. 327-341.

[13] Mary Ennis, The Elias Transcripts (© 1995 – 2001 by Mary Ennis and Vicki Pendley, © 2001–2006 by Mary Ennis), Elias Session 1105, June 8, 2002.

[14] Jane Roberts with Robert F. Butts , *Seth Speaks: The Eternal Validity of the Soul* (San Rafael, CA: Amber-Allen Publishing, 1994), p. 163, Session 546, Aug. 19, 1970.

[15] Jane Roberts with Robert F. Butts, *The Nature of Personal Reality: Specific, Practical Techniques for Solving Everyday Problems and Enriching the Life You Know (A Seth Book)* (San Rafael, CA: Amber-Allen Publishing, 1994), p. 45, Session 617, Sept. 25, 1972.

[16] Talbot, pp. 106-108.

[17] Byron Katie with Stephen Mitchell, *Loving What Is: Four Questions That Can Change Your Life* (New York, NY: Three Rivers Press, 2003).

[18] Louise L. Hay, *Heal Your Body: The Mental Causes for Physical Illness and the Metaphysical Way to Overcome Them* (Carlsbad, CA: Hay House, 1984).

[19] Hay, p. 62.

[20] Richard Bartlett, DC, ND, *Matrix Energetics: A Hands-on Guide to Subtle Energy and Radical Change* (New York, NY: Atria Books, 2007).

[21] Dr. Eric Pearl, *The Reconnection: Heal Others, Heal Yourself.* (Carlsbad, CA: Hay House, 2003).

[22] Mildred Carter and Tammy Weber, *Body Reflexology: Healing at Your Fingertips* (New York, NY: Penguin Group, 1994).

[23] Talbot, pp. 150-152.

[24] Peter Kelder, *Ancient Secret of the Fountain of Youth: Book 1* (New York, NY: Doubleday, 1998).

[25] Christopher S. Kilham, *The Five Tibetans: Five Dynamic Exercises for Health, Energy, and Personal Power* (Rochester, VT: Healing Arts Press, 1994).

[26] Ennis, Elias Digests – Energy Centers Appendix (compiled by Bobbi Houle), http://www.eliasforum.org.

[27] Ennis.

[28] Carter and Weber, pp. 297-301.

[29] Carole Maggio, *Carole Maggio Facercise®: The Dynamic Muscle-Toning Program for Renewed Vitality and a More Youthful Appearance* (New York, NY: Perigree Trade, 2002).

[30] Jacob Liberman, OD, PhD, *Light: Medicine of the Future* (Santa Fe, NM: Bear & Company, 1991), pp. 51 and 175-177.

[31] Carter and Weber, pp. 189.

[32] Jacob Liberman, OD, PhD, *Take Off Your Glasses and See: A Mind/Body Approach to Expanding Your Eyesight and Insight* (New York, NY, Crown Publishers, 1995).

[33] Henry David Thoreau, "Where I Lived and What I Lived For," *Walden; or, Life in the Woods* (orig. pub. 1854).

Glossary

Acupressure points (also known as **acupuncture points**) – precise locations on the body where energy is concentrated; the Chinese mapped these points over a 2,000-year period.

Acupressure (also see **reflexology**) – applying pressure to specific points on the surface of the body to increase energy, alleviate pain, and restore the body to optimal functioning.

Acupuncture – a traditional Chinese medical practice that involves the insertion of fine needles at precise points in the body to restore balance and treat health problems.

Acupuncture meridians – a network of energy channels throughout the body, on which various **acupuncture points** are located.

Anabolism – synthesis; rebuilding, and repair processes in living organisms.

Anthocyanins – **flavonoids** in plant pigments ranging from blue to violet to red; biologically active compounds that are powerful antioxidants with numerous health benefits.

Antioxidant – a substance that protects body cells from the damaging effects of oxidation, which is caused by **free radicals**.

Ayurveda (pronounced "eye-ur-vay-dah") – *ayur* means *life* and *veda* means *science* in Sanskrit; an ancient Indian system of holistic health.

Carnivore – an animal that eats mostly flesh foods.

Carotenoids – plant pigments ranging from yellow to orange to red; biologically active compounds that are powerful antioxidants with numerous health benefits.

Catabolism – breakdown processes in living organisms.

Chakra – means *wheel* or *disk* in Sanskrit; one of the nonphysical energy centers associated with the human body.

Cortisol – the major adrenal cortex hormone; it is active in protein and carbohydrate metabolism and is released in greater-than-usual quantities in response to stress.

Cosmetic acupuncture (also known as **facial rejuvenation acupuncture**) – the use of **acupuncture** techniques to revitalize facial skin tone and texture; reduce fine lines, wrinkles, puffiness, and loss of elasticity; and improve overall facial appearance.

Dehydroepiandosterone (DHEA) – a steroid hormone produced by the adrenal glands that can be converted to other steroid hormones; it is believed to counteract some of the biological effects of age-related degeneration.

Dental fluorosis – irregular calcification, mottling, weakness, and discoloration of teeth; caused by overexposure to fluoride while the teeth are developing.

Dermis – the lower, connective tissue layer of the skin that contains nerve endings, oil and sweat glands, and blood and lymph vessels.

Dissociative identity disorder (DID) – a mental condition in which a person has multiple distinct personalities that are not all aware of one another; formerly known as multiple personality disorder.

Effectors – cellular proteins that carry out cell behavior.

Ellagic acid – a phenolic compound with antimicrobial and anticancer properties; present in high concentrations in red raspberries, strawberries, and walnuts.

Emotional Freedom Techniques (EFT) – developed by Gary Craig; an energy psychology therapy that is a form of thought field therapy, which treats emotional problems by correcting energy field disruptions by tapping on **acupressure points** while the person being worked on "tunes in" to the problem being addressed.

Energy healing – restoring to a state of balance by means that affect the body's nonphysical energy centers and mind-body energy field.

Energy psychology – a collective description of the various therapies for addressing emotional issues based upon the premise that emotional problems are characterized by disruptions in the body's energy field, and that these problems can be treated with methods that affect the energy field.

Enucleated – with the nucleus removed.

Epidermis – the outer, protective layer of the skin.

Endorphins – peptide hormones that bind to opiate receptors (found primarily in the brain), reducing pain and increasing feelings of pleasure and comfort.

Facial tapping – a technique for stimulating **acupressure points** and improving circulation to the face; performed by using the fingertips to tap briskly all over the face and head.

Feng shui (pronounced "fung shway") – *feng* means *wind* and *shui* means *water* in Chinese; the Chinese art of placement, used for interior and exterior design of living areas.

Flavonoids – plant chemicals that are potent antioxidants with antimicrobial properties and numerous health benefits; includes the **anthocyanin** group.

Float tank (also known as a **flotation tank** or **isolation tank**) – developed in 1954 by John C. Lilly, MD; a lightproof, sound-insulated chamber that contains Epsom salt-infused water warmed to an average person's skin temperature; used for relaxation, deep meditation, and achieving altered states of consciousness.

Free radical – one or more atoms that have at least one unpaired electron; in the body, an oxygen molecule that has lost an electron and stabilizes itself by taking an electron from a nearby molecule, causing cell damage.

Genetically engineered foods – foods in which the genetic material has been modified to enhance specific traits such as growth rate, appearance, flavor, shelf life, or resistance to disease or pests.

Genetically modified organisms (GMOs) – an organism whose genetic material has been altered using genetic engineering techniques.

Global characteristics – patterns expressed in many diverse aspects of a person's life; examples include perfectionism, impulsiveness, procrastination, overindulgence, thoroughness, and neatness.

Glycemic index – related to the rise in blood glucose that results from eating a carbohydrate food.

Hatha yoga (pronounced "hat-ha yoga") – the branch of **yoga** that involves the practice of physical postures.

Herbivore – an animal that eats mostly plant foods.

Holistic – emphasizing the importance of the whole and the interdependence of its parts; the term is used to describe more natural alternatives to conventional medical therapies.

Integral membrane proteins (IMPs) – special cellular proteins; **receptors** and **effectors**.

Lutein – a plant chemical in the **carotenoid** family that is particularly beneficial for the eyes; present in high concentrations in bilberries, as well as kale, spinach, and other dark green leafy vegetables.

Lycopene – a plant chemical in the **carotenoid** family that is beneficial for the vascular system and has anticancer effects (particularly for prostate cancer); present in high concentrations in red vegetables and fruits.

Mahasamadhi – the Sanskrit term for a yoga master's final exit from the physical body.

Mantra – a word or phrase repeated in meditation, prayer, or incantation.

Matrix Energetics® – developed by Richard Bartlett, DC, ND; a system of healing, self-care, and transformation that is powered by intent, yields physical and observable effects, and is transferable and teachable.

Micronized – ground into tiny particles, as is done to the zinc oxide and titanium dioxide used in modern sunscreens.

Mindfulness – incorporating meditation into daily life by paying attention to what you are doing in the moment, without having extraneous thoughts.

Molecular distillation – a purification process in which a substance is heated under vacuum with such low pressure that no intermolecular collisions can occur before condensation.

Oil pulling – a holistic remedy developed in India that helps detoxify the teeth, gums, and body by removing mucous, bacteria, and toxins through the saliva; the technique involves placing a tablespoon of cold-pressed vegetable oil into the mouth and swishing and pulling it through the teeth for 15 to 20 minutes without swallowing.

Organelle – a structure within a cell that performs a differentiated function.

Palming – an eye relaxation technique performed by cupping the hands over closed eyes to block out as much light as possible.

Paradigm – a set of assumptions, concepts, values, and practices that constitutes a way of viewing reality.

Phospholipids – the major structural lipids (fats) of most cellular membranes.

Piezoelectric – the property of certain crystals that causes them to produce voltage when mechanical pressure (including sound vibrations) is applied.

Probiotics – beneficial bacteria (such as *L. acidophilus*, *B. bifidus*, and *L. reuteri*) that normally populate the intestines and are necessary for proper digestion.

PSYCH-K® – developed by Robert M. Williams, MA; an energy psychology therapy that works by increasing communication between the two brain hemispheres and facilitating direct communication with the subconscious mind, enabling people to alter their beliefs and maximize their potential.

Quantum mechanics – a theory in physics based on the principle that matter and energy have the properties of both particles and waves.

Quantum physics – the branch of physics that uses **quantum mechanics** theory to describe and predict the qualities of a physical system.

Qi gong (pronounced "chee gong" or "chee kung") – *qi* means b*reath of life* or *life force* and *gong* means "mental control of the body" in Chinese; an ancient Chinese discipline that stimulates the flow of life force energy by using controlled breathing and movements.

Receptors – cellular proteins that act as the "sense organs" of the cells.

Reconnective Healing – discovered by Eric Pearl, DC, a form of energy healing that accesses frequencies that return the body and mind to a state of balance.

Reflexology (also see **acupressure**)– a practice that involves applying pressure to specific points (commonly called **acupressure points**) on the surface of the body to increase energy, alleviate pain, and restore the body to optimal functioning; the term is most often used to refer specifically to pressure applied to the feet and hands.

Reiki (pronounced "ray-key") – *rei* means *the Higher Power* and *ki* means *life force energy* in Japanese; *reiki* means *spiritually guided life force energy*; developed by Dr. Mikao Usui, an energy therapy technique for healing and relaxation, administered by "laying on hands."

Tapas Acupressure Technique® **(TAT**®**)** – developed by Tapas Fleming, LAc; an energy psychology therapy that involves placing one's attention on an issue while touching a few specific **acupressure points** on the face and head; used for ending stress and allergic reactions; gaining self-confidence, and attaining empowerment.

Tapotement – a massage technique that involves using the fingertips to lightly tap areas of the face or body.

The Work® – developed by Byron Katie, a process of inquiry that teaches people to identify and question thoughts that cause suffering and to address their problems with clarity.

Therapeutic Touch – developed by Dolores Krieger, PhD, RN, with her mentor Dora Kunz; a method of energy therapy derived from the ancient practice of "laying on hands"; used extensively by nurses and healthcare practitioners worldwide.

Thought field therapy – developed by Roger Callahan, PhD; an energy psychology therapy that treats emotional problems by correcting energy field disruptions by tapping on **acupressure points** while the person being worked on "tunes in" to the problem being addressed.

Tibetan Rites of Rejuvenation (also known as the **Five Tibetans**) – believed to have originated in Tibet; a yoga-like exercise routine said to prevent aging by activating the body's nonphysical energy centers; consists of five basic rites plus an optional sixth rite.

Toning – using the human voice to release tensions and restore the body to a balanced, healthy state.

Triple-A process – a three-step method for dealing with negative feelings about something; the steps are Acknowledge, Address, and Abandon.

Vastu shastra – *vastu* means *site*, *building*, or *house* and *shastra* means *treatise* or *instruction*; the Hindu system of architectural design that involves designing and constructing living environments that are in harmony with natural forces.

Vegan – a diet that excludes all animal products (meat, fowl, fish, dairy, eggs, and honey).

Vegetarian – a diet that includes plant food and animal products such as dairy and eggs, but no flesh foods (meat, fowl, or fish).

Yoga – means *yoke* or *union* in Sanskrit; an ancient Indian art based on a harmonizing system of development for the mind, body, and spirit.

Zeaxanthin – a plant chemical in the **carotenoid** family that is particularly beneficial for the eyes; present in high concentrations in kale, spinach, and other dark green leafy vegetables.

Resources

Books

Richard Bartlett, DC, ND, *Matrix Energetics: A Hands-on Guide to Subtle Energy and Radical Change.* New York, NY: Atria Books, 2007.

Itzhak Bentov, *Stalking the Wild Pendulum: On the Mechanics of Consciousness.* Rochester, VT: Destiny Books, 1988.

Deepak Chopra, MD, *Ageless Body, Timeless Mind: The Quantum Alternative to Growing Old.* New York, NY: Harmony Books, 1994.

Alan Cohen, *I Had It All the Time: When Self-Improvement Gives Way to Ecstasy.* Makawao, HI: Alan Cohen Pub., 1994.

Byron Katie with Stephen Mitchell, *Loving What Is: Four Questions That Can Change Your Life.* New York, NY: Three Rivers Press, 2003.

Christopher S. Kilham, *The Five Tibetans: Five Dynamic Exercises for Health, Energy, and Personal Power.* Rochester, VT: Healing Arts Press, 1994.

Karen Kingston, *Clear Your Clutter with Feng Shui.* New York, NY: Broadway Books, 1999.

Jacob Liberman, OD, PhD, *Take Off Your Glasses and See: A Mind/Body Approach to Expanding Your Eyesight and Insight.* New York, NY: Crown Publishers, 1995.

Bruce Lipton, PhD, *The Biology of Belief: Unleashing the Power of Consciousness, Matter, and Miracles.* Santa Cruz, CA: Mountain of Love, 2005.

Jane Roberts with Robert F. Butts, *Seth Speaks: The Eternal Validity of the Soul*. San Rafael, CA: Amber-Allen Pub., 1994.

Jane Roberts with Robert F. Butts, *The Nature of Personal Reality: Specific, Practical Techniques for Solving Everyday Problems and Enriching the Life You Know (A Seth Book)*. San Rafael, CA: Amber-Allen Pub., 1994.

Michael Talbot, *The Holographic Universe*. New York, NY: Harper Perennial, 1992.

David Tate (compiled by), *The Shift: A Time of Change (An Elias Book)*. London, England: Contact Publishing, 2004.

Machaelle Small Wright, *Behaving as if the God in All Life Mattered*. Warrenton, VA: Perelandra Limited, 1997.

Machaelle Small Wright, *MAP: The Co-Creative White Brotherhood Medical Assistance Program*. Warrenton, VA: Perelandra Limited, 2006.

Websites

Bruce Lipton – brucelipton.com

Elias Forum – eliasforum.org

Elias Web – eliasweb.at

For additional information, see the *Transcend Aging* website, transcendaging.com.